FRENCH

BUSINESSMATE

compiled by
LEXUS
with
Nicole Marin

PARRAGON

First published 1983
by Richard Drew Publishing Ltd

This edition published in 1994 by
Parragon Book Service Ltd
Avonbridge Industrial Estate
Atlantic Road, Avonmouth
Bristol BS11 9QD

Printed and bound in Italy

YOUR BUSINESSMATE is specifically designed to be of maximum service to you on your business trip to France, Belgium or Switzerland (or if you are having French visitors here in Britain). The BUSINESSMATE gives you one single A–Z list of terms and expressions to help you communicate efficiently in French:

* at the sales meeting
* in discussions of terms, contracts, schedules
* in looking at figures and accounts
* in finding solutions and making plans

And in addition to this you'll find words and phrases that will be useful when you are

* travelling
* at your hotel
* coping with typical business trip problems

Built into the A–Z list, for speed and ease of reference, there are some 500 French words, French abbreviations and acronyms you'll find on documents, statements, balance sheets, invoices, notices etc. There is factual and practical information too: travel tips (see 'train', 'métro' etc), conversion tables (see 'foot', 'pint' etc), a menu reader (see 'menu'), a wine guide (see 'wine'), numbers on pp 188–189 and a map on p 8.

On pp 4 to 7 there are notes on the pronunciation of French and basic points about French grammar.

All in all, your BUSINESSMATE will make for a smoother, more efficient trip. If you are in business, then

this book means business!

The table below relates spelling to sounds, with English equivalents (notes 1 to 8, 10, 12) or French examples (notes 9, 11) given where appropriate; for items marked with *, see also A and B below; groups of letters shown here never cross syllable boundaries, ie. -aim as in 'faim', not 'ai-mer'; -ail as in 'travail', not 'ai-lier'.

a, â, à	[ah]	**-er**	[-ay]	**on/om**	[o̅n̅][3]
ai, aî	[ay]	**eu, eû**	[uh][4]	**ou, oû, où**	[oo]
-ail	[i][1]	**-ez**	[-ay]	**ou**	[w][9]
-ain/aim	[a̅n̅][2]	**g** (+e/i)	[j][5]	**qu**	[k]
-an/am	[o̅n̅][3]	**gn**	[ny][6]	**r**	[r][10]
au	[oh]	**h**	silent	**s***	[s]
ç, c (+e/i)	[s]	**i, î**	[ee]		[z]
ch	[sh]	**i**	[y][7]	**t***	[t]
e*	[uh][4]	**-in/în/im**	[a̅n̅][2]		[s][11]
silent or	[eh]	**j**	[j][5]	**th**	[t]
é	[ay]	**ll**	[l]	**u, û**	[ꝏ][12]
è, ê	[eh]		[y][7]	**u**	[w][9]
eau	[oh]	**o**	[oh]	**-un/um**	[a̅n̅][2]
ei	[ay]	**ô**	[oh]	**y**	[ee]
-eil	[ay]	**oe, oeu**	[uh][4]		[y][7]
-ein	[a̅n̅][2]	**oi, ois**	[wah]	**-yn/ym**	[a̅n̅][2]
-en/em	[o̅n̅][3]	**-oin**	[wa̅n̅][8]	**x***	[ks]

also: **-euil,** as in 'seuil' [suh-ee]
oeil [uh-ee], **yeux** [yuh]
Noël [noh-el]
maïs [mah-eess]

1. *i*ce (travail, travailler, bail)
2. mer*in*gue (demain, plein)
3. restaurant
4. *a*bove (le premier)

5. mea*s*ure (je, gêné)
6. o*ni*on (signer, montagne)
7. *y*et (paille, travailler, vieux)
8. w+'in' as in mer*in*gue (coin, coincé)
9. French oui [wee], ouate [wat]; suis [swee], huile [weel]
10. the 'r' is produced with the uvula (try gargling!)
11. as in French 'nation' [nass-yo̅n̅]
12. as in 'huge', 'dew' (rue, du)

A. When final, e, d, s, t and x are usually silent: 'usine' [ꝏ-zeen], gris [gree], chaud [ʒhoh], petit [puh-tee] etc; in feminine endings (when preceding 'e'), d, s, t are sounded: chaude [shohd], grise [greez], petite [puh-teet].

Sometimes d, s, t or x are sounded before an initial vowel in the following word (this is called 'liaison'): vous avez [voo*z* ah-vay], vous êtes [voo*z* ayt], aux Etats-Unis [oh*z* ay-tah*z* ꝏ-nee]; learn by listening carefully to French speakers.

B. -ain/-in *etc*+feminine ending: the nasal sound is lost; sain [sa̅n̅], but saine [sen]; un [a̅n̅], une [ꝏn]

HOW TO SPELL IN FRENCH

a [ah] **b** [bay] **c** [say] **d** [day] **e** [uh] **f** [eff] **g** [jay] **h** [ash] **i** [ee] **j** [jee] **k** [kah] **l** [el] **m** [emm] **n** [enn] **o** [oh] **p** [pay] **q** [kꝏ] **r** [airr] **s** [ess] **t** [tay] **u** [ꝏ] **v** [vay] **w** [doobluh-vay] **x** [eeks] **y** [ee-grek] **z** [zed]

If you are starting to learn French, or are using rusty school French at a business meeting, the greatest difficulties are likely to include the question of gender, and verb forms and tenses; here is some basic help with these problems.

1. Gender ('le' or 'la'?)
In the BUSINESSMATE we give you the article with every translation of a noun. Depending on the likely context of use, it'll be the French equivalent of either 'the' or 'a'. In some cases, you will also find 'du', 'de la' or plural 'des', for English 'some'.

If the article is 'le' (the) or 'un' (a, an), it means the noun is masculine; if it is 'la' or 'une', the noun is feminine. Where it is 'l'', as in 'l'avion', we specify the gender with *m* or *f*.

Remember that if you use an adjective with a noun, it should 'agree': un petit modèle, une petite usine; un ordinateur puissant, une machine puissante.

Also, articles are generally used even where you wouldn't have 'the' in English: 'I prefer plastic', but 'je préfère le plastique'.

Finally, remember that 'de' + 'le' is '**du**': la secrétaire du directeur (*the manager's secretary*); 'de' + 'les' is '**des**': les désirs des clients (*the customers' wishes*). Similarly, 'à' + 'le' becomes '**au**': je vais au bureau (*I'm going to the office*); and 'à' + 'les' is '**aux**': adressez-vous aux fabricants (*apply to the manufacturers*).

2. Verbs

The present tense of verbs will be sufficient to help you get by in most situations:

arriv**er** [ahree-vay]	to arrive
j'arrive [jah-reev]	I arrive
tu arriv**es** [tōō ah-reev]	you arrive
il arriv**e** [eel ah-reev]	he(it) arrives
elle arriv**e** [el ah-reev]	she(it) arrives
nous arriv**ons** [nooz ahree-vōn]	we arrive
vous arriv**ez** [vooz ahree-vay]	you arrive
ils arriv**ent** [eelz ah-reev]	they arrive
elles arriv**ent** [elz ah-reev]	they arrive

finir 'to finish': je finis /fee-nee/, tu finis, il(elle) finit /fee-nee/, nous finissons /feenee-son/, vous finissez /feenee-say/, ils finissent /fee-neess/

A number of verbs are irregular. Your A–Z BUSINESSMATE will give you the main forms you need to know under the entries for 'be', 'have', 'go' etc.

Finally, the past tense is generally made up with the 'auxiliary' have (avoir): j'ai payé (I paid, I have paid), il n'a pas payé (he didn't pay, he hasn't paid); some verbs take the auxiliary be (être): je suis allé (I went, I have been), il n'est pas allé (he hasn't been, he didn't go)

Good luck, and remember – if you do try to speak their language, however basic your proficiency, your French contacts will greatly appreciate it!

LA FRANCE
International Airport
Principal Railways
0 km 200
LA MER DU NORD
LA MANCHE
LE GOLFE DE GASCOGNE
LA MEDITERRANEE
L'ECOSSE
L'ANGLETERRE
LE PAYS DE GALLES
LA HOLLANDE
LA BELGIQUE
L'ALLEMAGNE
LA SUISSE
L'ITALIE
L'ESPAGNE
LA CORSE
Glasgow
Londres
Douvres
Amsterdam
Ostende
Calais
Boulogne
Bruxelles
Lille
Liège
Bonn
Luxembourg
Le Havre
Rouen
Reims
Metz
Caen
Paris
Nancy
Strasbourg
Brest
Rennes
Orléans
Besançon
Bâle
Berne
Nantes
Dijon
Lausanne
Poitiers
La Rochelle
Limoges
Clermont-Ferrand
Lyon
Genève
Bordeaux
Saint-Etienne
Grenoble
Turin
Nîmes
Montpellier
Bayonne
Toulouse
Pau
Marseille
Nice
Côte d'Azur
Barcelone
Madrid
Ajaccio
Rhin
Seine
Loire
Rhône
Les Alpes
Pyrénées

a, an un(une)
10 francs a litre 10 francs le litre
about: is he about? est-ce qu'il est là?
about 15 environ quinze
at about 2 o'clock vers deux heures
above au-dessus (de ...)
above that de plus
above-mentioned sus-mentionné(e)
abroad à l'étranger
accept accepter
acceptable acceptable
acceptance l'acceptation
acceptance trials essais avant l'acceptation
accès interdit *no entry*
accident: there's been an accident il y a eu un accident
» *TRAVEL TIP: if anybody is hurt, get the police; for minor accidents, make sure both parties sign the 'constat à l'amiable' (forms provided with your green card documents)*
accommodation: we need accommodation for three il nous faut de la place pour trois personnes
accordance: in accordance with conformément à
according: according to Mr. Duval selon M. Duval
according to the contract conformément au contrat
account (*bank*) un compte
(*bill*) la facture
(*customer*) le client
15% on account 15% d'acompte
that will be taken into account nous en tiendrons compte
account number le numéro de compte

---

accountant un comptable
accounting method la méthode comptable
accounting period l'exercice financier
accounts: **our accounts for the past year** nos comptes pour l'année passée
may we look at your accounts for 1983? pouvons-nous examiner votre comptabilité pour 1983?
accounts department la comptabilité, le service comptable
accurate précis(e)
accusé de réception *confirmation of receipt*
achat *buying, 'buy'*
achats *buying, purchases*
acknowledge reconnaître
acknowledge receipt of accuser réception de
across de l'autre côté (de ...)
across the board: **an across the board increase** une augmentation générale
actif *assets, 'employment of capital (or funds)'*
action *share (stock)*
actionnaire *shareholder*
actual *(as against targeted)* effectif(-ive)
actuary un actuaire
adaptor un adaptateur
add ajouter
additional supplémentaire
address une adresse
will you give me your address? pouvez-vous me donner votre adresse?
adequate qui convient, suffisant(e)
adjudication *sale by auction, award (to tenderer), invitation to tender*
adjust ajuster
administrateur *director (board member)*
administrateur délégué *managing director (board member)*
administration la gestion
admission *(to club)* l'entrée

adult un adulte
advance: in advance à l'avance
can we book in advance? est-ce qu'on peut réserver à l'avance?
advance payment paiement à l'avance
advantage un avantage
advertisement (*for a product*) une réclame (*for a job, a flat*) une annonce
I want to put an advertisement in the paper j'aimerais mettre une annonce dans le journal
advertising la publicité
advertising campaign une campagne publicitaire
advice: we would appreciate advice as to when ... veuillez nous faire savoir quand ...
advice note une note
payment advice un avis de paiement
advisable recommandé
advise: please advise us veuillez nous faire savoir
we have been advised that ... nous venons d'être informés que ...
affranchissement *postage, franking*
AFP Agence France Presse
afraid: I'm afraid I don't know je regrette, je ne sais pas
I'm afraid so c'est malheureusement le cas
I'm afraid not je crains que non
we are afraid that ... nous craignons que ..., nous avons peur que ...
after: after you après vous
after 2 o'clock après deux heures
afternoon l'après-midi
in the afternoon l'après-midi
good afternoon bonjour (Monsieur *etc*)

after sales service le service après-vente
again de nouveau
against: **against the dollar** par rapport au dollar
age l'âge *m*
it takes ages ça prend très longtemps
agency (*office*) une agence
(*distributorship*) la représentation
agency agreement un accord de représentation
we have sole agency for ... nous avons l'exclusivité pour la distribution de ...
agenda: **on the agenda** à l'ordre du jour
agent le représentant
AGM l'assemblée générale
ago: **a week ago** il y a une semaine
it wasn't long ago il n'y a pas longtemps de ça
how long ago was that? il y a combien de temps de ça?
agree: **I agree** je suis d'accord
I can't agree with that je ne suis pas d'accord avec ça
if we can agree on a solution si nous pouvons nous mettre d'accord
do you agree that this is too much? êtes-vous d'accord que c'est trop?
agreeable: **if you are agreeable** si vous voulez bien, si vous êtes d'accord
agreement: **we're in agreement on that** nous sommes d'accord sur ce point
let's try to reach an agreement essayons de nous mettre d'accord
you broke the agreement vous n'avez pas respecté notre accord
agrégé *holder of 'agrégation', diploma for teaching at university level*
aim (*of talks etc*) l'objectif *m*
air l'air *m*
by air en avion
by airmail par avion

airfreight le fret aérien
we'll airfreight them to you nous vous les expédierons par avion
airport l'aéroport *m*
air waybill la lettre de transport aérien
alarm: **give the alarm** donnez l'alarme
alarm clock un réveil
alcohol l'alcool
is it alcoholic? est-ce que c'est alcoolisé?
alerte *alarm*
all: **all the people** tout le monde
all night/all day toute la nuit/toute la journée
that's all wrong c'est entièrement faux
all right! d'accord!
that's all c'est tout
thank you — not at all merci — de rien
allocations *benefits*
allow permettre
will you allow us more time? pouvez-vous nous accorder un délai supplémentaire?
have you allowed for inflation? est-ce que vous avez prévu les effets de l'inflation?
allowance une indemnité
allowed: **is it allowed?** est-ce que c'est permis?
it's not allowed ce n'est pas permis, c'est interdit
allow me permettez-moi
almost presque
alone seul(e)
already déjà
also aussi
alter modifier, changer
alteration une modification
when we've carried out the alterations lorsque nous aurons effectué les modifications
although bien que

altogether ensemble, au total
always toujours
a.m. *see* **time**
ambassador l'ambassadeur *m* (l'ambassadrice *f*)
ambulance l'ambulance *f*
amende *fine*
amendment (*to contract etc*) une modification
America l'Amérique
American américain(e)
among parmi
amortissement *redemption, writing off*
amortissements *(reserves for) depreciation*
amount (*sum*) le montant
  the total amount le total, la somme totale
  it amounts to more than ... ça s'élève à plus de ...
analyse analyser
analysis l'analyse
and et
angry fâché(e)
  I'm very angry about it cela me contrarie beaucoup
  please don't get angry je vous en prie, ne vous fâchez pas
annexe *appendix, enclosure*
annonce *advertisement*
annoy: **it's very annoying** c'est très ennuyeux
annual annuel(le)
annual accounts le rapport financier de l'année
annual report le compte rendu annuel
another: **can we have another room?** est-ce qu'on peut avoir une autre chambre?
  another beer, please une autre bière, s'il vous plaît
ANPE Agence Nationale Pour l'Emploi: *state employment agency, Job Centre*
answer une réponse
  what was his answer? qu'est-ce qu'il a répondu?

any: **have you got any water/pepper/cigars?** avez-vous de l'eau/du poivre/des cigares?
I haven't got any je n'en ai pas
isn't there any chance? n'y a-t-il pas la moindre chance?
anybody n'importe qui
is anybody in? est-ce qu'il y a quelqu'un?
I don't know anybody je ne connais personne
anything n'importe quoi
have you got anything for ...? avez-vous quelque chose pour ...?
I don't want anything je ne veux rien
APEC Agence Pour l'Emploi des Cadres: *Professional and Executive Recruitment*
aperitif un apéritif
apologize s'excuser (**for** de)
apology des excuses
please accept my apologies veuillez m'excuser
I want an apology je demande des excuses
appel d'offres *invitation to tender*
appelé au remboursement le ... *called up for redemption on ...*
appendix (*to a contract*) une annexe
applicant un candidat (une candidate)
application form un formulaire d'inscription
apply: **to apply for** (*membership, licence*) faire une demande en vue d'obtenir
(*job*) faire acte de candidature pour
that doesn't apply in this case ce n'est pas valable dans ce cas
appointment un rendez-vous
can I make an appointment? est-ce que je peux fixer un rendez-vous?
I have an appointment j'ai rendez-vous
apports *assets brought in*

appreciate: **we appreciate your problem** nous comprenons votre problème
yes, I appreciate that, but ... oui, je vous comprends, mais ...
we would appreciate it if you could ... nous vous serions reconnaissants si vous pouviez ...
thank you, I appreciate it merci, je vous en suis reconnaissant
it actually appreciates in value en fait ça prend de la valeur
appreciation: **as a sign of our appreciation** en signe d'appréciation
approach: **you should approach our agents** vous devriez entrer en relation avec nos représentants
we have been approached by another firm nous avons été contactés par une autre firme
have they been making approaches to you? vous ont-ils pressentis?
our approach to distribution notre politique en matière de distribution
appropriate: **the appropriate department** le service compétent
at the appropriate time en temps voulu
approval l'accord
not without your approval pas sans votre accord
approve: **do you approve?** est-ce que vous êtes d'accord?
you have to approve these changes vous aurez à donner votre accord pour ces modifications
approximately environ
Appt. appartement: *flat*
appuyer *push*
après *after*
April: **in April** en avril
are *see* **be**
area la région

in the area dans les environs
area manager le directeur régional
arm le bras
around *see* **about**
arrange: will you arrange it? pouvez-vous arranger ça?
it's all arranged tout est en ordre
that's easily arranged ça peut s'arranger facilement
arrangement: we have a special arrangement with them nous avons conclu un arrangement particulier avec eux
can we discuss the arrangements? pouvons-nous discuter des dispositions?
all the arrangements have been made toutes les dispositions ont été prises
arrdt. arrondissement: *(Paris) district*
arrears: you have arrears of ... vous avez un arriéré de ...
payments are in arrears les paiements sont en retard
arrérages *arrears*
arrêt *stop*
arrêté *decree*
arrhes *deposit, down payment*
arriéré *payment overdue*
arrival l'arrivée
arrive: we only arrived yesterday nous ne sommes arrivés qu'hier
arrivée *arrival*
art l'art
artificial artificiel(le)
as: as quickly as you can aussi rapidement que vous pouvez
as much as you can autant que vous pouvez
as you like comme vous voulez

as of today à partir d'aujourd'hui
a.s.a.p. dans les plus brefs délais
ascenseur *lift*
ashtray un cendrier
ask demander
could you ask him to ...? pourriez-vous lui demander de ...?
that's not what I asked for ce n'est pas ce que j'ai demandé
I have been asked to tell you ... on m'a demandé de vous dire
asleep: **he's still asleep** il dort encore
aspirin une aspirine
assemblée générale *general meeting*
assembly *(of machine)* le montage
assembly instructions les instructions de montage
asset: **this would be a major asset** cela représenterait un atout considérable
assets (*on balance sheet*) l'actif *m*
assistant l'adjoint *m* (l'adjointe *f*)
(*shop*) le vendeur (la vendeuse)
assistant manager le directeur adjoint
assume: **I assume ...** je suppose ...
can we safely assume that ...? pouvons-nous admettre avec certitude que ...?
that's just an assumption ce n'est qu'une hypothèse
assurance: **you have my assurance that ...** soyez assuré que ...
assurance *insurance*
assure: **could you assure us that ...?** pourriez-vous nous assurer que ...?
rest assured je vous le garantis
at: **at the airport** à l'aéroport
at my hotel à mon hôtel
at one o'clock à une heure
ATA *temporary admission*
atmosphere l'atmosphère

attach joindre
the attached invoice la facture ci-jointe
attaché case un attaché case
attention: **for the attention of Mr ...** à l'attention de M ...
please pay special attention to ... veuillez noter tout particulièrement ...
thank you for bringing it to our attention merci de nous l'avoir fait remarquer
attention à ... *caution: ...*
attitude l'attitude *f*
attractive (*offer, price*) intéressant(e)
(*design, display*) attrayant(e), qui plaît
audit: **after last year's audit** après le contrôle des comptes de l'année écoulée
auditor un commissaire aux comptes
August: **in August** en août
Australia l'Australie
Australian australien(ne)
Austria l'Autriche
Austrian autrichien(ne)
authority: **I need my director's authority** il me faut l'autorisation de mon directeur
do we have your authority to ...? est-ce que nous avons votre autorisation pour ...?
authorities l'administration
authorize (*steps, decision*) autoriser
I'm not authorized to ... je n'ai pas qualité pour ...
automatic automatique
automatically automatiquement
autumn: **in the autumn** en automne
available (*goods*) disponible
(*person*) libre
on the next available flight par le premier vol possible

---

availability: **subject to availability** suivant disponibilité
avant *before*
avantages sociaux *social benefits*
average: **average results** résultats moyens
above/below average au-dessus/au-dessous de la moyenne
avertissement *warning*
avocat *solicitor, barrister, lawyer*
avoid: **to avoid delay** afin d'éviter tout retard
avoir *cash in hand, assets*
await: **we are awaiting ...** nous attendons ...
awaiting your prompt reply nous comptons sur une réponse immédiate
aware: **are you aware of the ...?** est-ce que vous vous rendez compte de ...?
away: **is it far away from here?** est-ce que c'est loin d'ici?
awful affreux(-euse)
back: **I'll be right back** je reviens tout de suite
is he back? est-ce qu'il est de retour?
when will he be back? quand est-ce qu'il revient?
can I have my money back? pouvez-vous me rendre mon argent?
come back revenez
I go back tomorrow je rentre demain
at the back derrière
we'll get back to you on that nous reprendrons contact avec vous à ce sujet
backer (*for scheme*) un commanditaire
backing: **we need your backing** nous avons besoin de votre soutien
backlog (*of work*) le travail en souffrance
(*of orders*) les commandes en souffrance
back out: **I'm afraid you can't back out** je regrette, vous ne pouvez pas vous dédire
they backed out at the last minute ils se sont dédits à la dernière minute

back up: **the figures back it up** les chiffres le prouvent
bad mauvais
too bad tant pis
bad debts des créances non recouvrables
baggage les bagages
bail *lease*
bain(s) *bath(s)*
balance (*money*) le solde
(*goods, etc*) le reste
on balance tout compte fait, l'un dans l'autre
balance out: **they balance each other out** ils s'équilibrent
balance sheet le bilan
ball-point pen un stylo à bille
bank la banque
bank account un compte bancaire
bank draft une traite bancaire
bank loan un prêt bancaire
bank manager un directeur d'agence
bankrupt en faillite
bar un bar
barber's le coiffeur
barême *price structure, tariff*
bargain: **it's a real bargain** c'est une bonne affaire
barmaid la serveuse
barman le barman
base: **our French base** notre établissement en France
it's based on the assumption that ... ceci présuppose que ...
based: **Paris-based** basé à Paris
basic (*problem*) fondamental, de base
basically: **we are basically interested** en principe nous sommes intéressés

---

it's basically the same c'est pratiquement la même chose
basis la base
as a basis for negotiations comme base de négociations
bath un bain
bathroom la salle de bains
I'd like a room with a private bathroom je voudrais une chambre avec salle de bains
battery une pile
bd. *boulevard*
be être
I am je suis, **we are** nous sommes
you are vous êtes, (*informal*) tu es
he/she is il/elle est, **it's** c'est; il/elle est
they are ils sont, **they aren't** ils ne sont pas
I was, you were *etc.* j'étais, vous étiez (*informal*: tu étais), il (elle) était, nous étions, ils étaient
he's been ill il a été malade
don't be late ne soyez pas en retard
be reasonable soyez raisonnable
beat: **to beat the competition** battre la concurrence
we can beat these prices nous pouvons battre ces prix
beautiful beau(belle)
because parce que
because of the delay à cause du retard
bed un lit
single bed un lit à une place
double bed un grand lit
twin beds des lits jumeaux
I'm off to bed je vais me coucher
bed and breakfast une chambre avec petit déjeûner
bedroom une chambre
beer de la bière
two beers, please deux bières, s'il vous plaît

» *TRAVEL TIP: for the equivalent of half-pint of draught lager ask for 'un demi pression'; the standard measure is 33 cl; if you simply ask for 'une bière' you may be served bottled beer (more expensive); in Switzerland, ask for 'une bière (pression)'*

before: **before breakfast** avant le petit déjeûner
before we leave avant de partir
I haven't been here before c'est la première fois que je viens ici

begin: **when does it begin?** quand est-ce que ça va commencer?

beginning le début, le commencement
beginning next month dès le début du mois prochain

behalf: **on behalf of Mr McGregor** au nom de M. McGregor
on behalf of our company pour le compte de notre société
on your/his behalf en votre/son nom

behind derrière
we're behind on delivery nous sommes en retard pour la livraison

Belgian belge
(*person*) un Belge (une Belge)

Belgium la Belgique

believe: **I don't believe you** je ne vous crois pas
I believe you je vous crois

belong: **that belongs to me** c'est à moi
who does this belong to? à qui est ceci?

below au-dessous de

bénéfice d'exploitation *trading profits*

bénéfices *profits*

BEPC Brevet Elémentaire: *school leaver's certificate*

---

berth (*on ship*) une couchette
beside à côté (de ...)
best le meilleur (la meilleure)
  we'll do our best nous ferons tout notre possible
  the best would be ... le mieux serait ...
better meilleur(e)
  haven't you got anything better? est-ce que vous n'avez rien de mieux?
  are you feeling better? est-ce que vous vous sentez mieux?
  I'm feeling a lot better je me sens beaucoup mieux
between entre
beyond plus loin que
bid une offre
big grand
  a big one un grand
  that's too big c'est trop grand
  it's not big enough ce n'est pas assez grand
  have you got a bigger one? est-ce que vous en avez un plus grand?
bilan *balance sheet(s)*
bill la note, l'addition *f*
  could I have the bill, please? pouvez-vous me donner l'addition, s'il vous plaît?
bill of exchange une traite
bill of lading un connaissement
billets *ticket office*
bit (*piece*) un morceau
  just a bit un peu
  that's a bit too expensive c'est un peu trop cher
black noir(e)
  in the black: this year we are in the black cette année le bilan est positif
blood le sang
  blood group le groupe sanguin
  high blood pressure de la tension

bloody mary une vodka tomate
blue bleu(e)
board (*of directors*) le conseil d'administration
board meeting la réunion du conseil
full board la pension complète
half board la demi-pension
boarding pass la carte d'embarquement
boat un bateau
bon de caisse *cash voucher*
bon de commande *purchase order*
bonded warehouse un entrepôt de douane
book un livre
can I book a seat for ...? est-ce que je peux réserver une place pour ...?
I'd like to book a seat for ... j'aimerais réserver une place pour ...
I'd like to book a table for two j'aimerais réserver une table pour deux
YOU MAY THEN HEAR ...
c'est à quel nom? *what is the name, please?*
c'est pour quelle heure? *for what time?*
booking office le guichet
books: your books votre comptabilité
bookshop une librarie
border la frontière
boring ennuyeux(-euse)
born: I was born in 1945/Glasgow je suis né en 1945/à Glasgow
borrow: can I borrow ...? est-ce que je peux emprunter ...?
borrowings les emprunts
boss le patron
both les deux
I'll take both of them je les prendrai tous les deux
bottle une bouteille

bottom: **at the bottom of the list** au bas de la liste
Bourse: la Bourse *the Stock Exchange*
box une boîte
(*au théâtre*) une loge
boy un garçon
BP Boîte Postale: *PO Box*
brake freiner
I had to brake suddenly j'ai dû freiner subitement
he didn't brake il n'a pas freiné
branch une succursale
branch manager un directeur de succursale
branch office une succursale
brand une marque
we must increase brand awareness il nous faut sensibiliser le public à la marque
brand image l'image de marque
brandy le cognac
brasserie *café-style restaurant, also serves snacks*
breach: **they are in breach of contract** ils ont rompu le contrat
bread du pain
could we have some bread and butter? est-ce que vous pouvez nous apporter du pain avec du beurre?
some more bread, please encore un peu de pain, s'il vous plaît
break (*contract, agreement*) rompre
breakdown (*car*) une panne
(*of figures, facts*) le détail
could you give me a full breakdown? (*figures*) pouvez-vous me faire le décompte détaillé?
(*facts*) pouvez-vous me faire une analyse détaillée?
break even équilibrer son budget
at that rate we don't even break even à ce

taux-là, nous ne rentrons même pas dans nos frais
breakeven point le seuil de rentabilité
breakfast le petit déjeûner
English breakfast le petit déjeûner à l'anglaise
brevet *patent*
briefcase un porte-documents, une serviette
briefing: please give me a full briefing on the situation faites-moi un rapport sur la situation
brilliant brillant(e)
bring apporter
could you bring it to my hotel? pourriez-vous l'apporter à mon hôtel?
bring forward: we've brought the date forward three weeks nous avons avancé la date de trois semaines
Britain la Grande-Bretagne
British britannique
the British les Britanniques
I'm British je suis britannique
brochure un prospectus
have you got any brochures about ...? avez-vous de la documentation sur ...?
broken: you've broken it vous l'avez cassé
my room/car has been broken into quelqu'un s'est introduit dans ma chambre/voiture
broker un courtier
brought forward le report
brown brun(e)
browse: can I just browse around? est-ce que je peux regarder?
brut *gross*
buffet un buffet

build construire
building un bâtiment
bunch of flowers un bouquet de fleurs
bunk une couchette
buoyant (*market*) soutenu(e), ferme
bus l'autobus *m*
bus stop l'arrêt d'autobus
could you tell me when we get there? est-ce que vous pouvez m'avertir quand on y arrive?
» *TRAVEL TIP: pay-as-you-enter in most cities; you can buy a 'carnet de tickets' (book of tickets) from a newsagent; in Geneva, Lausanne: ticket-vending machines at bus stop, ticket usu. valid for one hour (any number of trips); see also* **métro**
business les affaires
I'm here on business je suis ici pour affaires
business trip un voyage d'affaires
we have a business proposition to put to you nous avons une affaire à vous proposer
we look forward to doing more business with you nous espérons continuer à travailler avec vous
it's a pleasure to do business with you c'est un plaisir de traiter avec vous
our business relationship nos rapports en affaires
that's not our way of doing business ce n'est pas notre manière de traiter
business is business les affaires sont les affaires
bust: **to go bust** faire faillite
busy (*person, telephone*) occupé
we're very busy these days nous sommes très occupés ces jours-ci, nous avons beaucoup de travail ces jours-ci
butter du beurre
button un bouton
buvette *'refreshments'*

buy acheter
  where can I buy ...? où est-ce que je peux acheter ...?, **I'll buy it** je l'achète
  nobody's buying them personne n'en veut
  our company has been bought by ... notre société a été rachetée par ...
  we'll buy up the remaining stock nous rachèterons le reste du stock
buyer un acheteur(une acheteuse)
buying department le service des achats
by: **I'm here by myself** je suis venu seul
  can you do it by January? est-ce que vous pouvez le faire d'ici à janvier?
  by train/car/plane en train/voiture/avion
  by the station près de la gare
  who's it made by? c'est fabriqué par qui?
  signed/ordered by ... signé/commandé par ...
CA chiffre d'affaires: *turnover*
cabin une cabine
cabine téléphonique *telephone box*
cable (*message*) un câble
CAF (CIF) Coût Assurance Fret: *cost insurance freight*
cafe un café
café *the usual place for a drink or snack*
» *TRAVEL TIP: waiter service, but in France drinks cheaper at the bar; alcoholic drinks served all day; set lunch ('plat du jour') usually available; you can telephone from most 'cafés' and in France there is often a special counter where stamps and tobacco are sold; you generally pay for your drinks on leaving rather than on ordering*
caisse *cash desk, cashier*
cake un gâteau
calculator une calculatrice

call: **will you call the manager?** pourriez-vous appeler le gérant?
what is this called? comment ça s'appelle?
he'll be calling on you next week il passera vous voir la semaine prochaine
I'll call you back je vous rappellerai
see **telephone**
call box une cabine téléphonique
calm calme
calm down calmez-vous
camera un appareil-photo
campaign une campagne
can[1]: **a can of beer** une bière en boîte
can[2]: **can I have ...?** est-ce que je peux avoir ...?
can you ...? est-ce que vous pouvez ...?
I can't ... je ne peux pas
he can't ... il ne peut pas
we can't ... nous ne pouvons pas ...
can they ...? est-ce qu'ils peuvent ...?
Canada le Canada
Canadian canadien(ne)
cancel (*order*) annuler
I want to cancel my booking je veux annuler ma réservation
can we cancel dinner for tonight? est-ce que nous pouvons décommander le dîner de ce soir?
the flight has been cancelled le vol a été annulé
cancellation (*flight*) l'annulation
CAP Certificat d'Aptitude Professionnelle: *awarded after trade apprenticeship*
capacity la contenance
capital (*money*) le capital
capital equipment les immobilisations
capital expenditure les dépenses en investissements
capital-intensive qui nécessite un investissement important
capital social *authorized capital*

capitaux permanents *fixed assets*
car une voiture
carafe une carafe
card: **business card** une carte de visite
do you have a card? avez-vous une carte de visite?
care: **will you take care of my briefcase for me?** est-ce que je peux vous confier mon porte-documents?
careful: **be careful** soyez prudent(e)
car-ferry un ferry
cargo la cargaison
car park un parking
carriage forward port dû
carriage free franco de port
carriage paid port payé
carrier le transporteur
carry: **will you carry this for me?** est-ce que vous pouvez me porter ça?
carry forward reporter
carry on continuer
please carry on as before veuillez continuer comme auparavant
carry out: **it wasn't properly carried out** ça n'a pas été exécuté correctement
we've carried out your request votre ordre a été exécuté
carton un carton
case (*suitcase*) une valise
(*packing case*) une caisse
in that case dans ce cas
as the case may be suivant le cas
an isolated case un cas isolé
in such cases dans ces cas-là
he has a good case ses arguments sont valables

cash (*pay*) comptant
in cash en espèces
I haven't any cash je n'ai pas de liquide
cash desk la caisse
will you cash a cheque for me? pouvez-vous me payer ce chèque?
cash flow la trésorerie, le cash flow
cash flow forecast une prévision de trésorerie
cash flow problems les problèmes de trésorerie
cassette une cassette
catch: **where do we catch the bus?** où est-ce qu'on prend le bus?
cater for: **to cater for your special needs** pour répondre à vos besoins particuliers
cause: **the cause of the trouble** la cause des difficultés
it's caused a bit of inconvenience ça a occasionné quelques difficultés
caution *guarantee*
c/c compte courant: *current account*
CC Corps Consulaire
CCP Compte Chèques Postaux: *Giro cheque account*
CD Corps Diplomatique
CE Comité d'Entreprise: *works committee*
CEDEX Courrier d'Entreprise à Distribution Exceptionnelle: *centralized sorting office for business mail, in main cities*
CEE Communauté Economique Européenne: *EEC*
ceiling (*limit*) un plafond
up to a ceiling of jusqu' à un maximum de
cellophane la cellophane
centigrade centigrade
» *to convert C to F* : $C \div 5 \times 9 + 32 = F$

centigrade	–5	0	10	15	21	30	36.9
Fahrenheit	23	32	50	59	70	86	98.4

centimetre un centimètre
» *1 cm=0.39 inches*

central central
centre le centre
certain: **are you certain?** est-ce que vous êtes certain?
please make certain that ... veuillez vous assurer que ...
I'll make certain (*check*) je m'en assurerai
certificate un certificat
C et F coût et fret: *cost and freight*
CFDT Confédération Française et Démocratique du Travail: *a major association of trade unions in France*
CFF Chemins de fer Fédéraux: *the Swiss Railways*
CFTC Confédération Française des Travailleurs Chrétiens: *Christian assoc. of trade unions, in France*
CGC Confédération Générale des Cadres: *association of managerial employees, in France*
CGT/FO Confédération Générale du Travail/ Force Ouvrière: *a major association of trade unions (communist), in France*
CH Confédération Helvétique: *on number plates: Switzerland*
chainstore une succursale de grand magasin, un magasin à succursales multiples
chair une chaise
(*armchair*) un fauteuil
(*at meeting*): **he was in the chair** il présidait
chairman le président
chairwoman la présidente
chambermaid la femme de chambre
chambres disponibles *rooms to let*
champagne du champagne
chance: **just one more chance** donnez-nous encore une chance

it's an excellent chance to ... c'est une excellente occasion de ...
change: **could you change this into francs?** est-ce que vous pouvez me changer ça en francs?
I haven't got the right change je n'ai pas la monnaie
do you have change of 10 francs? est-ce que vous avez la monnaie de dix francs?
do we have to change trains? est-ce qu'il faut changer?
I'd like to change my booking/flight etc j'aimerais changer de réservation/vol
it can't be changed now on ne peut plus changer maintenant
there are going to be a lot of changes il va y avoir beaucoup de changements
three changes to the contract specifications trois modifications aux termes du contrat
keep us informed of any changes in the situation tenez-nous au courant de tout changement de situation
change *foreign exchange, bureau de change*
channel: **the Channel** la Manche
chaque *each, every*
charge: **what do you charge?** combien est-ce que ça coûte?
who's in charge? qui est le responsable?
charge it up mettez-le sur la facture
it'll be charged to your account nous débiterons votre compte
who do I charge it to? à qui faut-il envoyer la facture?
what are the charges? cą revient à combien?
no extra charge sans supplément
charges *costs, expenses*
chart (*flow chart etc*) un graphique
chartered accountant un expert-comptable

chaussée verglacée *ice (on road)*
cheap bon marché
check: **will you check the total?** pouvez-vous vérifier le total?
I've checked j'ai vérifié
we checked in/we checked out at 10 nous sommes arrivés/partis à dix heures
have you checked your facts? avez-vous vérifié vos données?
I'll check it out je vais vérifier
detailed checks have shown that ... des contrôles minutieux ont montré que ...
regular checks will be carried out des contrôles réguliers seront exécutés
checklist une checklist
chef le chef cuisinier
chemist's une pharmacie
cheque un chèque
will you take a cheque? est-ce que vous acceptez un chèque?
cheque book un carnet de chèques
cheque card une carte d'identité bancaire
chèques postaux *Giro accounts*
chest la poitrine
chiffre d'affaires *turnover*
children les enfants
chocolate du chocolat
choice: **a wider choice of products** un choix plus large de produits
we have no choice nous n'avons pas le choix
choose choisir
Christian name le prénom
» *TRAVEL TIP: use of Christian name is not standard practice in business; best let the French speaker take the initiative*
Christmas: **at Christmas** à Noël

---

au [oh], ç [s], ch [sh], e [uh, eh], é [ay], è [eh], eau [oh] -er [-ay], eu [er], -ez [-ay], gn [ny], i [ee], ou [oo], qu [k] y [ee]; *see also pp 4–5*

cider du cidre
Cie compagnie: ... *and Company*
c.i.f. CAF
cigar un cigare
cigarette une cigarette
cinema un cinéma
circular circulaire
(*letter*) une circulaire
circulation sur une voie *one-way traffic*
circumstances: **under no circumstances** en aucun cas
in the circumstances dans ces circonstances-là, dans le cas présent
city une ville
claim: **our claim against the carrier** notre réclamation contre le transporteur
the claims we make for our product les qualités que nous revendiquons pour notre produit
we intend to claim damages nous avons l'intention de réclamer des dommages et intérêts
clarify clarifier
clarification une mise au point
clean (*not dirty*) propre
(*to wash etc*) nettoyer
clear clair(e)
I'm not clear about it je n'ai pas bien compris
I want to make this perfectly clear je voudrais que ce soit parfaitement clair
I'd be grateful if you would clear it up je vous serais obligé de bien vouloir éclaircir cette question
when they're cleared through Customs lorsqu'ils (elles) seront dédouané(e)s
clearance (*Customs*) les formalités de douane
clearing bank la chambre de compensation
clerk un employé (une employée)
clerical error une erreur d'écriture

clever intelligent(e)
client un client (une cliente)
cloakroom le vestiaire
(*WC*) les toilettes
clock une horloge
close[1]: is it close? est-ce que c'est près d'ici?
close[2]: when do you close? quand est-ce que vous fermez?
close down (*business*) fermer
closed fermé(e)
cloth le tissu
clothes les vêtements
CNPF Conseil National du Patronat Français: *equivalent to CBI*
CNRS Centre National de la Recherche Scientifique
co- co-
c/o c/o
coach un autocar
coat un manteau
c.o.d. comptant à la livraison
coffee un café
two coffees, please deux cafés, s'il vous plaît
» *TRAVEL TIP: white coffee as you know it is not served; 'café au lait' is hot milk with hot black coffee; 'café crème' is black coffee with a drop of milk or cream; if you want black coffee, simply ask for 'un café' (small: 'petite tasse', large: 'grande tasse'); in Switzerland, 'un renversé' is the same as 'café au lait'; for expresso coffee, ask for 'un express'*
coin une pièce de monnaie
coincidence une coincidence
cold froid
I'm cold j'ai froid
I've got a cold j'ai un rhume

---

colis *parcels*
collaboration la collaboration
collar le col
colleague un(une) collègue
collect: I want to collect ... je viens chercher ...
to call collect téléphoner en PCV
collection (*of debts*) le recouvrement
bill for collection un effet à l'encaissement
colour une couleur
have you any other colours? est-ce que vous avez d'autres couleurs?
comb un peigne
come venir
I/we come from London je viens/nous venons de Londres
we came here last year nous sommes venus ici l'année dernière
when is he/are they coming? quand est-ce qu'il vient/qu'ils viennent?
come in! entrez!
come on! allons!
if we come to an agreement si nous arrivons à nous entendre, si nous parvenons à un accord
when are you next coming to see us? quand est-ce que vous reviendrez nous voir?
comfortable confortable
commande *order*
comments des commentaires
do you have any further comments? avez-vous quelque chose à ajouter?
commerçant *tradesman*
commerce le commerce
commercial commercial
commissariat *police station*
commission une commission
commission agent un représentant à la commission
on a commission basis au pourcentage
commit: we're fully committed to this project

nous nous sommes totalement engagés dans ce projet
we've committed a lot of time/money to this project nous avons investi beaucoup de temps/d'argent dans ce projet
you don't have to commit yourself vous n'avez pas à vous engager
I can't commit myself now je ne peux pas m'engager maintenant
commitment: our financial commitments nos engagements financiers
committee le comité
committee meeting une réunion de comité
Common Market le Marché Commun
company une société
company car une voiture de fonction
company report le rapport de gestion de la société
company secretary le secrétaire général
compare comparer
as compared with comparé à, en comparaison de
compensation un dédommagement
I demand compensation je demande un dédommagement
compete rivaliser avec, faire concurrence à
we can't compete with these prices nous ne pouvons rivaliser avec ces prix
competent compétent(e)
I'm not competent to deal with that je ne suis pas qualifié pour m'occuper de ça
competition la concurrence
strong competition une forte concurrence
competitive (*prices, product*) concurrentiel
competitors: our competitors nos concurrents
complain se plaindre

complaint une réclamation
complet *full, no vacancies*
complete: **is work complete?** est-ce que le travail est terminé?
the complete range la gamme complète
completely complètement
completion: **on completion of the work** à la fin du travail
complicated: **it's very complicated** c'est très compliqué
compliment: **my compliments to the chef** mes compliments au chef
comply: **in order to comply with your requests** afin de nous conformer à vos souhaits
component un composant
composter: prière de composter votre billet *please punch your ticket here*
compris *included, inclusive*
compte courant *current account*
compte livret *deposit account*
compte d'exploitation générale *trading account*
compte de pertes et profits *profit and loss account*
compte de régularisation *reconciliation statement*
compte de résultats *general accounts*
computer un ordinateur
computerized informatisé(e)
concern: **we were very concerned to hear this** ceci nous préoccupe
as far as we are concerned quant à nous
concerning your letter en ce qui concerne votre lettre
concession une concession
concessionaire un concessionnaire
conclusion: **what's your conclusion?** quelle est votre conclusion?
we must draw the appropriate conclusions

il nous faut en tirer les conclusions qui s'imposent
conclusive concluant(e)
condition: it's not in very good condition ce n'est pas en très bon état
conditional acceptance une acceptation sous réserve
conditionnement *packaging*
conference une conférence
conference room (*in hotel*) une salle de conférence
confidence: we have confidence in ... nous avons confiance en ...
this is in confidence c'est confidentiel
confidential: this is strictly confidential ceci est strictement confidentiel
confirm confirmer
confirmation la confirmation
we look forward to receiving confirmation of nous espérons recevoir la confirmation de
confirmed letter of credit une lettre de crédit confirmée
conformity: it is not in conformity with ce n'est pas conforme à
confuse: you're confusing me vous m'embrouillez!
congé *holiday*
congratulations! félicitations!
connaissement *bill of lading*
connection (*train*) la correspondance
connoisseur un connaisseur
conscious conscient(e)
conseil *consultant, board*
conseil d'administration *board of directors*
consent: do we have your consent? est-ce que nous avons votre accord?

consequence la conséquence
as a consequence of this en conséquence
consider: **we are considering the possibility of ...** nous envisageons la possibilité de ...
please ask him to consider it demandez-lui de bien vouloir examiner ça
have you considered making any changes? est-ce que vous pensez changer quelque chose?
it's worth considering ça vaut la peine d'y penser
considering its age étant donné son âge
all things considered tout bien considéré
consideration: **on consideration of ...** en tenant compte de ...
after due consideration of après mûre réflexion
consigne *left luggage office*
consigne automatique *left luggage lockers*
consignee le destinataire
consigner l'expéditeur *m*
consignment l'envoi *m*
consignment note le bon d'expédition
consommation *consumption*
consul le consul
consulate le consulat
consult: **I have to consult with ...** je dois consulter ...
consultancy: **consultancy business** un bureau conseil
consultancy fees des honoraires d'expert
our rates for consultancy nos tarifs de consultation
consultant un expert conseil
consultation la consultation
(*discussion*) la délibération
consumer le consommateur (la consommatrice)
consumer goods les biens de consommation
consumer needs les besoins du consommateur
contact: **how can I contact ...?** comment est-ce

que je peux contacter ...?
I'll get in contact soon (with ...) je me mettrai bientôt en rapport (avec ...)
please do not hesitate to contact us n'hésitez pas à nous contacter
that was a useful contact ceci a été un contact utile
he has useful contacts il a des relations utiles
container un conteneur
container base une base de conteneurs
contentieux *legal department, litigation*
contract un contrat
under the terms of the contract conformément aux termes du contrat
contrat d'exclusivité *sole agency agreement*
contravention *fine (for traffic offence etc)*
contribution (*to project etc*) la collaboration (*financial*) la contribution
control: under our control sous notre contrôle
everything is under control tout se passe bien
the necessary management control les procédures de contrôle
due to circumstances beyond our control en raison de circonstances indépendantes de notre volonté
controlling factor le facteur déterminant
convenience: at your earliest convenience dans les meilleurs délais
convenient pratique
is it convenient for you? est-ce que ça vous convient?
convince: I want to convince you that ... je voudrais vous persuader que ...
convocation *invitation to attend*

---

au [oh], ç [s], ch [sh], e [uh, eh], é [ay], è [eh], eau [oh] -er [-ay], eu [er], -ez [-ay], gn [ny], i [ee], ou [oo], qu [k] y [ee]; *see also pp 4–5*

cook: **it's not cooked** ce n'est pas cuit
cool frais(fraîche)
cooperate coopérer, collaborer
cooperation la coopération, le concours
cope: **can you cope with the extra demand?** est-ce que vous pouvez faire face à la demande supplémentaire?
copie *copy, carbon copy*
copy: **3 copies** trois exemplaires
we'll send you a copy (*of book*) nous vous en enverrons un exemplaire
please copy head office veuillez faire parvenir un double au siège
corner (*on road*) un virage
can we have a corner table? est-ce qu'on peut avoir une table d'angle?
corner the market accaparer le marché
correct correct(e)
correspond to (*relate*) correspondre à
correspondence la correspondance
cost: **what does it cost?** combien ça coûte?
our costs nos frais
at cost à prix coûtant
it's been carefully costed les coûts en ont été évalués avec soin
cost analysis l'analyse des coûts
cost-conscious: **we must be cost-conscious** nous ne devons pas perdre de vue la rentabilité
cost-effective rentable
cost estimate le devis
costing l'évaluation du coût
cost price le prix de revient
coté *quoted*
cotisation *contribution, membership fee*
cotton du coton
cotton wool du coton hydrophile
couchette une couchette
could: **could you please ...?** est-ce que vous pouvez ...?

could I have ...? est-ce que je peux avoir ...?
we couldn't ... nous n'avons pas pu ...
we could try nous pourrions essayer
country un pays
couple: **a couple of ...** quelques
courier: **by courier** par courrier spécial
cours *rate (of exchange); course (of lectures)*
course: **in the course of the meeting** au cours de la réunion
in the course of the next 3 months au courant des trois prochains mois
of course bien sûr
court: **I'll take you to court** je vous poursuivrai en justice
cover: **to cover our costs** couvrir nos frais
insurance cover la garantie, les risques couverts
cover charge le couvert
covering letter une lettre explicative
crate une caisse
crazy fou(folle)
créance *'credit', sum owed*
créancier *creditor*
credit: **we are in credit** notre compte est approvisionné
to the credit of your account au credit de votre compte
the bank is willing to grant us credit/ extend our credit la banque nous consent un crédit/une rallonge de crédit
on the credit side au crédit
please credit to the following account ... veuillez créditer le compte suivant ...
we are today crediting to you the sum of ... nous créditons aujourd'hui votre compte de la somme de ...

---

credit card la carte de crédit
credit facilities des facilités de crédit
credit note la note de crédit
credit terms les conditions de crédit
creditor le créancier
credit references des références
credit-worthy solvable
crisis la crise
critical path analysis un organigramme de production (analyse du 'chemin critique')
criticism une critique
we have one criticism nous avons une critique à formuler
criticize critiquer
cross: **our letters must have crossed in the post** nos lettres ont dû se croiser
CRS Compagnies Républicaines de Sécurité: *state police for emergencies, riots etc*
cup une tasse
a cup of coffee une tasse de café
current actuel(le)
the current month le mois en cours
current account un compte courant
current assets l'actif de roulement
current earnings les revenus actuels
current liabilities le passif exigible
currency la monnaie
in foreign currency en devises étrangères
curriculum vitae un curriculum vitae
customer un client(une cliente)
customer complaint une réclamation (d'un client)
customer service les rapports avec la clientèle
custom-made fait(e) sur commande
Customs la douane
Customs Authorities le service des douanes
Customs clearance le dédouanement
Customs duty un droit de douane
cut: **to cut costs** réduire les coûts

job cuts des réductions de personnel
there have been cuts all round il y a eu des compressions générales
cutback une diminution
CV Cheval Vapeur: *horsepower;* Curriculum Vitae
damage: we'll pay for the damage nous paierons les dégâts
it's damaged c'est abîmé
damaged in transit détérioré/endommagé en cours de transport
damages les dommages et intérêts
dames ladies
Dane un Danois(une Danoise)
dangerous dangereux(-euse)
Danish danois(e)
dark foncé(e)
data les données
data processing le traitement des données
date: what's the date? quelle est la date d'aujourd'hui?
can we fix a date? est-ce que nous pouvons fixer un rendez-vous?
on the first of June le premier juin
on the fifth of May le cinq mai
in 1984 en 1984
» *except for the 1st of the month use 'deux', 'trois' etc, and not 'deuxième' etc.; see numbers pp 188*
date of invoicing la date de facturation
to date we have not ... à ce jour nous n'avons pas ...
date limite deadline
day un jour
dead mort(e)
deadline la date limite
if we make the deadline si nous y arrivons

dans les délais
if we miss the deadline si nous dépassons la date limite
deadlock l'impasse
deal (*business*) un contrat, un marché
but we made a deal mais nous nous étions entendus/mis d'accord
it's a deal marché conclu!, d'accord!
I think we have a deal j'ai l'impression que l'affaire est conclue
will you deal with it? pouvez-vous vous en charger?
we don't deal in ... nous ne faisons pas le commerce de ...
dealer le fournisseur, le distributeur
dealership le contrat de distribution (d'un concessionnaire, d'une agence)
dear (*expensive*) cher(chère)
Dear Mr Dupont, ... Cher Monsieur, ...
Dear François, ... Cher François, ...
Dear Sir, ... Monsieur, ...
see also **letter**
debentures les obligations
debit: **a debit of £1,000** un débit de mille livres
on the debit side au débit
we have debited you with ... nous avons débité votre compte de ...
please debit our account veuillez débiter notre compte
débiteur *debtor*
debt une dette
December: **in December** en décembre
déchargement *unloading, offloading*
decide: **we have decided to ...** nous avons décidé de ...
we've decided on ... nous nous sommes décidés pour ...
that hasn't been decided yet ça n'a pas encore été décidé

decision une décision
we need a decision today la décision doit être prise aujourd'hui
decision-maker celui qui décide, un décideur
declare: **nothing to declare** rien à déclarer
découvert *overdraft*
decrease (*in sales etc*) une baisse
deep profond(e)
defect un défaut
defective défectueux(-euse)
defendant un accusé (une accusée)
(*in civil cases*) un défendeur (une défenderesse)
défense de fumer *no smoking*
deficit un déficit
definite précis(e)
it's not definite yet ce n'est pas encore certain
definitely certainement, sans aucun doute
definitely not certainement pas
déjeuner d'affaires *business lunch*
délai: dernier délai *deadline*
dans les délais *within the time limit*
delay le retard
the flight was delayed le vol a eu du retard
deliberately exprès
delicate délicat(e)
delicious délicieux(-euse)
deliver: **when can you deliver?** quand est-ce que vous pourrez livrer?
delivery (*of goods*) la livraison
to take delivery of ... prendre livraison de ...
delivery date la date de livraison
what sort of delivery are you looking for? quels délais de livraison désirez-vous?
is there another mail delivery? est-ce qu'il y a une autre distribution?
de luxe de luxe

demand (*for goods*) la demande
  (not) in demand (peu) demandé(e)
demonstration (*of gadget*) une démonstration
Denmark le Danemark
dentist un dentiste
deny: **I deny it** je ne l'admets pas
départ usine *ex works*
department store un grand magasin
départs *departures*
departure le départ
depend: **it depends** ça dépend
  it depends on him ça dépend de lui
  you can depend on it vous pouvez compter dessus
deposit un acompte
  do I have to leave a deposit? est-ce qu'il faut verser un acompte?
deposit account un compte d'épargne
depot un dépôt
depreciation la dépréciation
  (*in books*) l'amortissement
dépréciation *loss of value, depreciation*
depressed (*market*) déprimé
déranger: ne pas déranger *do not disturb*
describe décrire
description une description
desirable: **it would be desirable if ...** il serait souhaitable que ...
dessert un dessert
destinataire *addressee*
destination la destination
détail *retail (trade)*
detail un détail
  let's discuss the details voyons les détails de près
  I want to study this in detail j'aimerais étudier ça en détail
  a detailed account un rapport détaillé
detour un détour

dettes *debts*
devalued dévalué(e)
develop (*a business*) développer
a developing market un marché en expansion
development (*of business*) l'expansion *f*
recent development un développement récent
an unexpected development un événement inattendu
development grant une subvention de développement
déviation *diversion*
devis *quotation, estimate*
devises *currency*
diagram un diagramme
dialling code l'indicatif
dialling tone la tonalité
diamond un diamant
diary un agenda
dictating machine un dictaphone
dictionary un dictionnaire
diesel (*fuel*) du gas-oil
diet un régime
I'm on a diet je suis au régime
difference une différence
the price difference la différence de prix
the main difference with our arrangement is ... ce qui change par rapport à notre arrangement c'est ...
it doesn't make any difference cela ne change rien
different: **they are different** ils sont différents
can I have a different room? est-ce que je peux avoir une autre chambre?
is there a different route? est-ce qu'il y a un

autre itinéraire?
differently différemment
difficult difficile
difficulty une difficulté
we're having difficulties with ... nous avons quelques difficultés avec ...
dining room la salle à manger
dinner (*evening*) le dîner
dinner jacket un smoking
direct direct(e)
does it go direct? est-ce que c'est direct?
if they want to buy direct from us s'ils préfèrent acheter directement
direct debit un ordre de prélèvement automatique
direction la direction
the direction in which things are moving la tournure que prennent les événements
follow the directions suivez les indications
director un directeur, un administrateur
directory un annuaire
dirty sale
disadvantage un désavantage
disappear disparaître
disappointing décevant(e)
discount une réduction
cash discount une remise de caisse
discreet: **please be discreet** soyez discret
discrepancy une contradiction
discretion: **we'll leave it to your discretion** nous laisserons ça à votre discrétion
at your discretion à votre bon vouloir
discuss discuter
discussion la discussion
dishonest malhonnête
dispatch expédier
they'll be ready for dispatch ils seront prêts à l'expédition
dispatch date la date d'expédition

dispatch note le bordereau d'expédition
display pack un emballage présentoir
distance la distance
  in the distance au loin
distribution la distribution
distribution network le réseau de distribution
distribution rights les droits de distribution
distributor le distributeur
distributor discount la remise au distributeur
distributorship le contrat de distribution
disturb: **the noise is disturbing** le bruit nous dérange
divers *sundry, sundries*
dividend un dividende
divorced divorcé(e)
do faire
  how do you do? bonjour (Monsieur *etc*)
  what are you doing tonight? qu'est-ce que vous faites ce soir?
  how do you do it? comment est-ce que vous faites?
  I've never done it before je n'ai jamais fait ça
  we're doing everything we can nous faisons tout notre possible
  what are you doing about it? qu'est-ce que vous comptez faire?
  it won't do ça ne marchera pas, ça ne va pas
  don't, didn't *see* **not**
docket une fiche, un bordereau
doctor un docteur
  I need a doctor j'ai besoin d'un docteur
document un document
documentary credit le crédit documentaire
documentation une documentation
dollar le dollar
domicile: à domicile *at home, home*

DOM-TOM Domaines et Territoires d'Outre-Mer: *Overseas Territories*
door la porte
dotation à ... *appropriation to ...*
douane *Customs*
double: double room une chambre pour deux
double-whisky un double whisky
at double the cost deux fois plus cher
double-check vérifier
douche(s) *showers*
down en bas
sales are down on last year les ventes ont baissé par rapport à l'an dernier
to keep/get costs down maintenir/réduire les coûts
sales are down 15% les ventes ont baissé de 15%
downmarket bas de gamme
down payment un acompte
dozen une douzaine
half a dozen une demi-douzaine
draft (*bill of exchange*) une traite
(*of contract etc*) un projet
draft agreement un projet de contrat
drastic radical(e)
draw (*money*) retirer
a bill drawn on ... une traite sur
drawback un inconvénient
drawee le tiré
drawer le tireur
drawing (*plan etc*) un schéma, un croquis
draw up (*documents*) rédiger
incorrectly drawn up mal rédigé
dress une robe
drink: would you like a drink? désirez-vous boire quelque chose?
I don't drink je ne bois pas d'alcool
drive conduire
I've been driving all day j'ai roulé toute la

journée
you drive a hard bargain vous êtes dur en affaires
» *TRAVEL TIP: remember flashing headlights doesn't normally mean 'after you'; in France, pay attention to 'priorité': as a rule cars coming from the right have right of way unless you are in a 'passage protégé'; on roundabouts, let cars coming from the right go first, even when you are on the roundabout*
driver le conducteur (la conductrice)
driving licence le permis de conduire
drop: **a drop in sales/output** une baisse dans les ventes/la production
drunk ivre
dry sec (sèche)
dry-clean nettoyer à sec
dry-cleaner's un pressing
due: **when is the bus due?** quand est-ce que le bus arrive?
the next payment is due on ... le prochain paiement est attendu le ...
it falls due ... il (elle) vient à échéance le ...
due to ... dû à ...
in due course en temps utile
during pendant
Dutch hollandais(e)
dutiable passible de droit(s), taxable
duty (*import etc*) une taxe, un droit
duty-free hors taxes
dynamique dynamique
dz. douzaine: *dozen*
each: **can we have one each?** est-ce que nous pouvons en avoir un chacun?
how much are they each? combien coûte la pièce?

early tôt
we want to leave a day earlier nous voulons partir un jour plus tôt
next month at the earliest le mois prochain au plus tôt
east l'est
East Germany l'Allemagne de l'Est
Easter: **at Easter** à Pâques
easy facile
eat: **something to eat** quelque chose à manger
échantillon *sample*
échéance *expiry (date), maturity (date)*
economic économique
economic forecast les prévisions économiques
economy: **the economy** l'économie
EDF Electricité de France: *the French Electricity Board*
EEC le Marché Commun
EEC subsidies les subventions du Marché Commun
effect (*consequence*) l'effet
it comes into effect cela entre en vigueur
with immediate effect avec effet immédiat
with effect as of next month avec effet à partir du mois prochain
no longer in effect plus en vigueur
effective (*measures*) efficace
effectively (*in effect*) en fait
effet *draft, bill*
efficiency efficacité
efficient efficace
effort un effort
thank you for your efforts merci pour vos efforts
we shall spare no effort nous ferons tout notre possible
EFTA l'AELE (Association Européenne de Libre Echange)
e.g. par exemple

Eire l'Irlande
either: **either ... or ...** ou ... ou ...
I don't like either je n'aime ni l'un ni l'autre
elastic élastique
elastic band un élastique
electric électrique
electrician un électricien
electricity l'électricité *f*
electronic électronique
elegant élégant(e)
else: **something else** quelque chose d'autre
let's go somewhere else allons ailleurs
who else? qui d'autre?
or else ou alors
emballage *packing, packaging*
embarrassing gênant(e)
embarrassed gêné(e)
embassy l'ambassade *f*
emergency une urgence
» *emergency numbers on all telephone dials; 'Pompiers' fire brigade; 'Police Secours' police and ambulance*
émettre, émis, émission *to issue, issued, issue*
emphasis: **we put the emphasis on ...** nous mettons l'accent sur ...
emphasize souligner
employee un employé(une employée)
employer l'employeur *m*
employment l'emploi *m*
the people in your employment vos employés
to create employment créer des emplois
emprunt *loan, borrowing*
empty vide
ENA Ecole Nationale d'Administration: *prestige school for civil servants*

encaissé *paid-in (dividend)*
encaisser *to cash in*
enclose: **I enclose with my letter ...** je joins à ma lettre ...
enclosed: **please find enclosed ...** veuillez trouver ci-joint ...
the enclosed cheque le chèque ci-joint
end la fin
when does it end? quand est-ce que cela finit?
engaged occupé(e)
engagement: **a prior engagement** un engagement antérieur
engagements *undertakings*
engine un moteur
engineer un ingénieur
engineering l'ingénierie *f*
very advanced engineering une technologie de pointe
some engineering problems des problèmes techniques
England l'Angleterre *f*
English anglais(e)
the English les Anglais
I'm English je suis anglais(e)
enormous énorme
enough assez (de ...)
not big enough pas assez grand
not enough money pas assez d'argent
thank you, that's enough merci, cela suffit
enquête *inquiry*
enquire: **I'll enquire** je vais me renseigner
enquiry une demande de renseignements
could you make enquiries? pouvez-vous vous renseigner?
enregistrement *check-in (desk); registering; recording*
ensure: please ensure that ... veuillez vous assurer que ...
entail: **this will entail ...** cela va impliquer ...

entente *agreement*
entertainment: what is there in the way of entertainment in the evenings? qu'est-ce qu'il y a d'intéressant à faire le soir?
entertainment allowance une indemnité de frais de représentation
entitle: you will be entitled to ... vous aurez droit à ...
entrance l'entrée *f*
entrée libre *admission free*
entry l'entrée *f*
(*in books*) une écriture
envelope une enveloppe
envisage: do you envisage any immediate changes? est-ce que vous envisagez des changements immédiats?
equipment le matériel
electrical equipment une installation électrique
equities les actions
equity les capitaux propres
equivalent: that is the equivalent of ... c'est l'équivalent de ...
error une erreur
sent to you in error qui vous a été envoyé par erreur
escaliers *stairs*
escompte *discount*
especially spécialement
essential essentiel(le)
it is essential that ... il est essentiel que ...
establish: we have established that ... nous savons maintenant que ...
estimate (*quotation*) un devis
what's your estimate? quel est votre estimation?

---

we estimate that ... nous estimons que ...
we estimate it at ... nous l'évaluons à ...
estimated costs l'estimation des coûts
sales estimate la prévision des ventes
état-civil: ... *status: ... (single, married etc)*
Europe l'Europe
European européen(ne)
even: even the British même les Britanniques
evening: in the evening le soir
good evening bonsoir (Monsieur *etc*)
this evening ce soir
evening dress (*woman's*) une robe de soirée
is it an evening dress occasion? est-ce que le smoking est de rigueur?
éventualités *contingencies*
ever: have you ever been to ...? êtes-vous déjà allé à ...?
every chaque
every day chaque jour
everyone chacun
is everyone here? est-ce que tout le monde est là?
everything tout
everything we've tried tout ce que nous avons essayé
everywhere partout
evidence une preuve, des preuves
a piece of evidence une preuve
exact exact
exactly exactement
exactly! précisément!
example un exemple
for example par exemple
exceed dépasser
not exceeding £500 ne dépassant pas £500
excellent excellent(e)
except excepté, sauf
exception une exception
as an exception exceptionnellement

we can't make any exceptions nous ne pouvons faire d'exception
excess (*insurance*) la franchise
excess baggage un excédent de bagages
excess fare un supplément
exchange (*money*) le change
(*telephone*) le central
a useful exchange of ideas un échange d'idées utile
exchange rate le taux de change
exciting (*idea, enterprise*) très intéressante, passionnante
exclusivité *sole agency*
excuse: **excuse me** pardon Monsieur (*or* Madame, Mademoiselle)
I offer no excuses je n'ai pas à m'excuser
executive un cadre
senior executive un cadre supérieur
executive case un attaché-case
exercice financier *(current) financial year*
ex factory départ usine
ex gratia payment paiement à titre de faveur
exhausted épuisé(e)
exhibition une exposition
exhibitor un exposant
exit la sortie
expect attendre
we didn't expect that nous ne nous attendions pas à cela
larger than expected plus grand que prévu
expéditeur *sender*
expéditions *despatch*
expenditure la dépense, les dépenses
expense une dépense, des frais
at your/our expense à vos/nos frais
it's on expenses ça va sur la note de frais

expense account les frais de représentation
expensive cher(chère)
experience l'expérience
  in our experience dans notre expérience
experienced expérimenté(e)
experiment une expérience
expert un expert
expire: **it expires next month** il(elle) prend fin le mois prochain
expiry: **the expiry of the contract** l'expiration du contrat
expiry date la date d'expiration
explain expliquer
  would you explain that slowly? pourriez-vous expliquer cela plus lentement?
explanation une explication
exploitation *trading, operating*
export (*noun*) l'exportation *f*
  (*verb*) exporter
export director le directeur des exportations
export documents les documents d'exportation
export drive une relance des exportations
export licence la licence d'exportation
export manager le responsable des exportations
exposition *exhibition*
experimental: **an experimental model** un modèle expérimental
express (*send*) par exprès
extend (*deadline*) prolonger
  an extension of the deadline une prolongation du délai
extra supplémentaire
  an extra cost un coût supplémentaire
  an extra month un mois de plus
  is that extra? est-ce que c'est en supplément?
extrait de compte *statement of account*
extremely extrêmement
ex warehouse départ entrepôt
ex works départ usine

F Francs (français)
fabricant *manufacturer*
fabrique *factory, works*
face le visage
facility: **we don't have the facilities to ...** nous ne sommes pas équipés pour ...
facsimile *see* **fax**
fact un fait
fact-finding tour une voyage d'étude
factor (*element*) un facteur
factsheet un descriptif
factory une usine
facturation *invoicing*
facture *invoice*
Fahrenheit Fahrenheit
» *to convert F to C : F−32×5÷9=C*

Fahrenheit	*23*	*32*	*50*	*59*	*70*	*86*	*98.4*
centigrade	*–5*	*0*	*10*	*15*	*21*	*30*	*36.9*

fail: **if we fail to meet the targets** si nous n'arrivons pas à atteindre les objectifs
failing: **failing that** à défaut
faillite *bankrupcy*
failure un échec
failure rate le taux d'échec
faint: **she's fainted** elle s'est évanouie
fair[1] une foire
  book fair la foire du livre
fair[2] juste, équitable
  that's not fair ce n'est pas juste
faithfully: **yours faithfully** salutations distinguées; *see also* **letter**
fake un faux
fall tomber
  prices/sales are falling les prix/ventes sont en baisse
  falling demand une demande en baisse, une

diminution de la demande
output fell to ... la production est tombée à ...
we can always fall back on ... on peut toujours se rabattre sur ...
false faux(fausse)
famous réputé(e)
fan (*electric*) le ventilateur
far loin
is it far? est-ce que c'est loin?
how far is it? c'est à quelle distance d'ici?
fare le prix du billet
FAS *free alongside*
f.a.s. FAS
fascinating passionnant(e)
fashion la mode
fast rapide
don't speak so fast ne parlez pas si vite
fault un défaut
it's not our fault ce n'est pas de notre faute
faulty défectueux(-euse)
favour: **credit in your/our favour** le crédit en votre/notre faveur
we would favour ... notre préférence irait à ...
favourable (*conditions, terms*) favorable
we look forward to a favourable reply dans l'attente d'une réponse favorable
if we get a favourable reaction s'ils répondent favorablement
fax: **by fax** par télécopieur
favourite préféré(e), favori(te)
our favourite method notre méthode favorite
feature (*of product*) une caractéristique
one of the main features of ... l'un des traits principaux de ...
February: **in February** en février
fee (*for licence etc*) une redevance
(*consultant's*) les honoraires *m*
what's your fee? combien demandez-vous?
feedback une réaction, un feedback

could you give us some feedback? faites-nous part de vos réactions
feel: **I feel certain** j'en suis sûr
I feel tired je suis fatigué
I don't feel well je ne me sens pas très bien
I feel like ... j'ai envie de ...
felt-tip pen un stylo feutre
fermé *closed*
fermeture *closure*
ferry le ferry-boat
fetch: **will you come and fetch me?** est-ce que vous pouvez venir me chercher?
few peu (de ...)
few people peu de gens
only a few seulement quelques-uns
a few days quelques jours
fewer than moins de
FF Francs français
fiasco un fiasco
fiche *card, record*
fichier *file*
field: **our people in the field** nos spécialistes sur le terrain
in the field of ... dans le domaine de ...
fieldwork une enquête sur le terrain
fierce (*competition*) acharné(e)
fifty-fifty fifty-fifty, à cinquante pour cent
figure un chiffre
let's look at the figures examinons les chiffres
the figures are quite clear les chiffres parlent d'eux-mêmes
sales figures les chiffres de vente
file (*folder, box file etc*) un classeur
(*index*) un fichier
(*report*) un dossier

they're not on file ils ne sont pas fichés
filiale *subsidiary*
fill remplir
to fill in a form remplir un formulaire
film un film
fin *end*
final final(e), définitif(-ive)
final demand un dernier rappel
final offer une dernière proposition
final draft un projet définitif
finalize mettre au point
we're still finalizing our plans nous mettons la dernière main à notre plan
another fortnight to finalize matters encore une quinzaine avant que tout soit réglé
finance (*a project*) financer
extra finance des crédits supplémentaires
finance director le directeur des finances
financial financier
the financial aspect l'aspect financier
financial assistance une aide financière
it makes financial sense financièrement parlant, c'est valable
the last financial year l'exercice financier de l'année écoulée
financially financièrement
financially sound financièrement sain
find trouver
if you find it ... si vous le(la) trouvez
I've found a ... j'ai trouvé un ...
fine: **a 50 francs fine** une amende de 50 francs
OK, that's fine d'accord, ça va bien
finish: **I haven't finished** je n'ai pas fini
well/poorly finished goods des produits dont la finition est bonne/médiocre
Finland la Finlande
Finnish finlandais(e)
fire un incendie
fire! au feu!

he's been fired il a été licencié
firm (*enterprise*) une société
a firm offer une proposition ferme
a firm order une commande ferme
we need firmer control un contrôle plus strict est nécessaire
firm up: **we want to firm up this contract** nous désirons confirmer cet accord
first premier(-ière)
I was first j'étais le premier
at our first meeting lors de notre première rencontre
in the first place en premier lieu
at first d'abord
first class première classe
first name le prénom
fisc *tax authorities*
fit: **not fit for use** pas utilisable
we'll fit a new part nous allons adapter une nouvelle pièce
it doesn't fit cela ne va pas
can you fit us in tomorrow? est-ce qu'il vous serait possible de nous voir demain?
fix (*arrange, repair*) arranger
(*date, meeting*) fixer
flat (*apartment*) un appartement
(*not bumpy etc*) plat(e)
flat rate un tarif forfaitaire, un tarif unique
flavour la saveur
flexible adaptable
flight number le numéro de vol
float (*the pound*) faire flotter
floor l'étage *m*
on the second floor au deuxième étage
floppy disk un disque souple, une disquette
flourishing prospère, florissant(e)

flow: the flow of work le déroulement du travail
flowchart un graphique d'évolution
flower une fleur
flu la grippe
fluctuations des fluctuations
fluent: he speaks fluent French il parle français couramment
FMI Fonds Monétaire International: *IMF*
f.o.b. FOB
foggy brumeux(-euse)
foire *fair*
folder une chemise, un classeur
follow suivre
follow the instructions suivez les instructions
we'll follow it up nous y donnerons suite
would you follow this up? pourriez-vous en assurer le suivi?
follow-up: what sort of follow-up are you planning? que comptez-vous faire ensuite?
follow-up publicity la publicité de relance
fondé de pouvoir *authorized signatory/representative*
fonds de roulement *working capital*
fonds propres *stockholders' equity*
food la nourriture
food poisoning une intoxication alimentaire
fool un(e) imbécile
foot le pied
» *1 foot=30.1 cm=0.3 metres*
f.o.r. franco wagon
for pour
(*during*) pendant
for 3 months now depuis maintenant trois mois
valid for 3 years valable 3 ans
I'm for the idea je suis tout à fait pour
forbidden défendu(e)

forecast: **our production forecast** nos prévisions en matière de production
the forecast sales level le montant prévisionnel des ventes
foreign étranger(-ère)
foreign exchange le change
foreign exchange market le marché du change
foreigner un étranger(une étrangère)
foresee prévoir
forfait *(all-in) package, fixed price contract*
forget oublier
I've forgotten j'ai oublié
don't forget n'oubliez pas
fork une fourchette
form (*document*) un formulaire
formal officiel(le)
formal acceptance l'acceptation officielle
formal agreement un accord en bonne et due forme
format le format
in a new format dans un nouveau format
former: **the former arrangement** le précédent arrangement
the former ... the latter celui-là ..., celui-ci
formula une formule
formulaire *form*
forthcoming (*visit etc*) à venir
fortnight une quinzaine
fortunately heureusement
forward en avant
forwarding address l'adresse de réexpédition
could you forward my mail? pouvez-vous faire suivre mon courrier?
forwarding agent un transitaire
forwarding instructions les indications concernant l'expédition

found (*a company*) fonder
fournisseur *supplier*
fournitures *supplies*
FPA Formation Professionnelle des Adultes: *state-run adult training scheme*
Fr.s., Fr.b. Francs (suisses ou belges)
fragile fragile
frais de bureau *office costs*
frais d'établissement *capital expenditure*
frais de fabrication *production costs*
frais généraux *overheads*
framework (*for agreement*) le cadre
  within the framework of dans le cadre de
franco de port *carriage free*
franco wagon *FOR/FOT*
frappez avant d'entrer *please knock before entering*
France la France
franchise le contrat de franchise
frank: **I'll be frank** je serai franc(franche)
fraud la fraude
freak (*result etc*) exceptionnel(le) (par sa rareté)
free libre
  (*free of charge*) gratuit(e)
  admission free entrée libre
  when will he be free? quand est-ce qu'il sera libre?
  one free in every twelve ordered un exemplaire gratuit sur douze à la commande
  free port un port franc
  free sample un échantillon gratuit
freelance indépendant(e)
freight le fret
freight charges les frais de transport
freight collect paiement à l'enlèvement chez le transitaire
freight forwarder un transitaire
French français(e)
  (*person*) un Français(une Française)

I don't speak French je ne parle pas français
frequent fréquent(e)
fret freight
Friday vendredi
friend un ami(une amie)
friendly sympathique
from de
from England d'Angleterre
where is it from? d'où est-ce que ça vient?
from the 14th June à partir du 14 juin
from then on à partir de ce moment
from £250 à partir de £250
front (*of building*) le devant
in front (of) devant
in the front à l'avant
10% up front 10% d'avance
how much up-front cash? combien d'avance?
frontière border
fruitful (*talks*) fructueux(-euse), profitable
frustrating déprimant(e)
fulfill (*conditions*) remplir
full plein(e)
full-time (*work*) à temps plein
fumeurs smokers
function (*role*) la fonction
fun: **it's fun** c'est amusant
fundamental fondamental(e)
funny drôle
furniture les meubles
further plus loin
further information des renseignements complémentaires
for further details write to ... pour de plus amples détails, écrire à ...
further to your letter of ... comme suite à/en référence à votre lettre du ...

fusion *merger*
future futur(e)
  in future à l'avenir
futures (*shares*) des actions à terme
gain: **a gain of 15%** une augmentation de 15%
gallon un gallon
» *1 gallon=4.55 litres*
gamble: **it's a gamble** c'est un risque à prendre
gap (*in market*) un créneau
garage un garage
» *TRAVEL TIP: ask for 'un devis' (estimate), 'une facture détaillée' (itemized bill)*
gare SNCF *main station*
gas le gaz
GDF Gaz de France: *the French Gas Board*
gear l'équipement *m*, le matériel
  (*in engine*) une vitesse
general général(e)
general manager le directeur général
generally généralement
generate (*demand*) susciter, créer
generous généreux(-euse)
genius un génie
gentleman un monsieur [muhss-yuh]
gentleman's agreement un gentleman's agreement
gents les toilettes (pour messieurs)
genuine véritable
gérant *manager*
German allemand(e)
  (*person*) un Allemand(une Allemande)
  the Germans les Allemands
Germany l'Allemagne
gestion *management, running (of ...)*
gesture un geste
get: **will you get me a ...?** pouvez-vous me chercher ...?
  how do I get to ...? comment peut-on aller à ...?

where do I get off? où dois-je descendre?
where do you get your supplies? où est-ce que vous vous approvisionnez?
you can't get them any cheaper vous ne pouvez pas les avoir moins cher
where did you get it from? où l'avez-vous trouvé?
I'll get him to look at it je vais lui demander de l'examiner
we're not getting anywhere nous n'avançons pas
get back: **when can I get it back?** quand pourrai-je le(la) ravoir?, quand me le(la) rendrez-vous?
when do we get back? quand revenons-nous?
I'll get back to you je reprendrai contact
gift un cadeau
gilt-edged shares des valeurs de premier choix
gin du gin
gin and tonic un gin and tonic
girl une fille
giro: **postal giro** le service de chèques postaux
bank giro (le système de) virement bancaire
giro cheque un chèque de virement
give donner
I gave it to him je le lui ai donné
could you give us ...? pourriez-vous nous donner ...?
I'm practically giving it away vous l'avez pratiquement pour rien
glad content(e)
we were glad to hear that ... nous avons été heureux d'apprendre que ...
glass un verre, le verre
a glass of water un verre d'eau
glasses les lunettes

glue de la colle
GNP le PNB (Produit National Brut)
go aller
I am going there tomorrow j'y vais demain
he's going to Paris next month il va à Paris le mois prochain
we/they are going together nous y allons/ils y vont ensemble
where are you going? où allez-vous?
I went there last week j'y suis allé la semaine dernière
I'm going to check je vais vérifier
it goes against our policy cela va à l'encontre de notre politique
when does the train go? quand est-ce que le train part?
he's/it's gone il est parti
it's going well/badly ça marche bien/mal
go ahead: **we intend to go ahead with ...** nous avons l'intention de mettre à exécution ...
if you give us the go-ahead si vous nous donnez le feu vert
go along: **I'll go along with that** je serais d'accord avec ça
go back on: **you're going back on what you said/what we agreed** vous revenez sur ce que vous avez dit/sur notre accord
go down (*costs, sales*) baisser, diminuer
they're going down big in the UK ils marchent très fort en Grande-Bretagne
go for: **we should be going for 20%** nous devrions nous fixer 20% comme objectif
go into: **let's go into this in detail** examinons cela en détail
go on: **if things go on like this** si ça continue de cette façon
go over: **I want to go over the plans/results** je voudrais examiner les plans/les résultats
go through: **let's go through the figures/plans**

again reprenons les chiffres/les plans
go up (*prices*) monter
goal (*objective*) l'objectif *m*
gold l'or *m*
gold standard l'étalon-or *m*
golf le golf
good bon(ne)
good! très bien!
goodbye au revoir
goods les marchandises
goodwill (*of business*) le fonds de commerce
go-slow la grève du zèle
government le gouvernement
grace: **period of grace** des jours de grâce
grade (*of goods*) le calibre, la catégorie
gradually peu à peu
gramme un gramme
» *100 grammes=approx 3½ oz*
grant: **we can grant an extension of ...** nous pouvons accorder une prolongation de ...
to grant somebody credit accorder un credit à quelqu'un
government grants des subventions d'état
grateful reconnaissant(e)
I'm very grateful to you je vous suis très reconnaissant
gratitude la reconnaissance
gratuit *free*
great grand(e)
(*very good*) excellent
great! parfait!
Greece la Grèce
Greek grec (grecque)
greedy gourmand(e)
green vert(e)
grey gris(e)

grim (*outlook, meeting*) désagréable, déprimant(e)
gros *wholesale (trade)*
gross brut(e)
gross margin la marge brute
gross profit le bénéfice brut
ground: **to help you get this off the ground** pour vous aider à démarrer
on the ground par terre
on the ground floor au rez-de-chaussée
grounds: **we have grounds for complaint** nous avons des sujets de mécontentement
groundwork le travail de préparation
group un groupe
grow croître
a growing company une société en expansion
growth la croissance
a growth industry une industrie en pleine croissance
guarantee une garantie
(*surety*) une caution
is there a guarantee? est-ce qu'il y a une garantie?
it's guaranteed for 2 years c'est garanti deux ans
I can guarantee that je peux vous l'assurer
guaranteed loan un prêt garanti
guest un invité(une invitée)
guess deviner
at a guess I'd say ... au jugé, je dirais ...
it's just a guess c'est une conjecture, sans plus
guesstimate un calcul au 'pifomètre'
guichet *desk, booking office*
guide un guide
guidelines des directives *f*
guilty coupable
Gulf: **the Gulf** le Golfe (persique)
hair les cheveux
is there a hairdresser's here? est-ce qu'il y a

un coiffeur ici?
half la moitié
in the first half of 1984 dans la première moitié de 1984
for the past half year pendant les six derniers mois
half-yearly semestriel(le)
at half price à moitié prix
half the size deux fois plus petit
we need half as much again il nous faut une fois et demie cela
one and a half un et demi
hall d'entrée *lobby*
hand la main
it has been put in hand on s'en occupe
with everything to hand avec tout à portée de main
the job's in safe hands l'affaire est en mains sûres
handbag un sac à main
handicapés *disabled*
handkerchief un mouchoir
handle la poignée
we can handle that nous pouvons nous en charger
who handled the order? qui s'est occupé de la commande?
handle with care manipuler avec soin
handling charge frais de manutention
damaged in handling détérioré lors de la manutention
hand luggage les bagages à main
handmade fait à la main
handy (*gadget*) pratique
hangover la gueule de bois
happen: **I don't know how it happened** je ne

sais pas comment c'est arrivé
what's happening? qu'est-ce qui se passe?
what happened? qu'est-ce qui s'est passé?
happy heureux(-euse)
we would be happy to do ... c'est avec plaisir que nous ferions ...
hard dur(e)
hardly à peine
hard sell une vente agressive
hardware le matériel
harm: **it can't do any harm (to ...)** cela ne peut pas faire de mal (à ...)
harmonious harmonieux(-euse)
hate: **I hate ...** je déteste ...
I hate to have to tell you, but ... je suis désolé d'avoir à vous le dire, mais ...
have avoir
I have no time je n'ai pas le temps
he has no time il n'a pas le temps
we/they have enough money nous avons/ils ont assez d'argent
do you have any ideas? est-ce que vous avez une idée?, (*informal*) est-ce que tu as une idée?
I had, you had *etc* j'avais, vous aviez (*informal*: tu avais), il(elle) avait, nous avions, ils avaient
we've had problems nous avons eu des difficultés
can I have some water? est-ce que je peux avoir de l'eau?
I have to leave tomorrow je dois partir demain
when can you let us have it by? quand est-ce que vous pouvez nous le faire parvenir?
I'll have it sent je le ferai expédier
to have something done faire faire quelque chose
he il
head la tête

the person heading up the team/the operation la personne qui dirige l'équipe/l'opération
the head of this department le chef de ce service
headache un mal de tête
head office le siège social
headquarters le bureau central
health la santé
your health! à votre santé!
hear entendre
we have heard that ... nous avons appris que ...
hear, hear! voilà qui est parlé!
heart attack une crise cardiaque
heat la chaleur
heated (*discussion*) animé(e)
heating le chauffage
heavily (*overdrawn etc*) sérieusement
heavy lourd(e)
HEC Hautes Etudes Commerciales: *a major business school*
hedge: as a hedge against inflation comme protection contre l'inflation
height la hauteur
hello bonjour
help aider
can you help us? est-ce que vous pouvez nous aider?
if you need any help si vous avez besoin d'aide
help! à l'aide!
helpful utile
(*person*) obligeant(e)
her: I know her je la connais
give her ... donnez-lui ...

will you give it to her? est-ce que vous pouvez le(la) lui donner?
it's her c'est elle
see also **my**
here ici
come here venez ici
hesitate hésiter
please don't hesitate to get in touch n'hésitez pas à nous contacter
heures d'ouverture/fermeture *opening/closing times*
heures supplémentaires *overtime*
hide cacher
no hidden extras pas de surprises (c'est tout compris)
high haut(e)
higher plus haut
the highest offer l'offre la plus élevée
high-level (*talks*) de haut niveau
high-powered très important(e)
hill une colline
(*on road*) une côte
him: **I know him** je le connais
give him ... donnez-lui ...
will you give it to him? est-ce que vous pouvez le(la) lui donner?
it's him c'est lui
hindsight: **with hindsight** rétrospectivement, avec le recul
hire *see* **rent**
hire purchase l'achat à crédit, la vente à tempérament
his *see* **my**
history l'histoire *f*
hit (*car etc*) heurter
we've been badly hit by ... nous avons été sérieusement affectés par ...
hitch: **there's been a slight hitch** il y a eu une petite anicroche

hive off (*department*) décentraliser
HLM Habitations à Loyers Modérés: *council homes*
hold tenir
hold this tenez ça
they hold 15% of the shares ils détiennent 15% du capital
hold up: **production has been held up** la production a subi des retards
sorry, I was held up excusez-moi, j'ai été retenu
hole un trou
holiday les vacances
next Monday is a holiday lundi prochain est férié
closed for the summer holiday fermé pendant les vacances d'été
I'll be on holiday je serai en vacances
see **public holiday**
Holland la Hollande
home: **at home** chez moi (*or* chez nous *etc*)
my home address mon adresse personnelle
the home market le marché intérieur
home sales les ventes sur le marché intérieur
when we get home quand nous rentrerons
hommes *men, gents'*
honest honnête
honestly? vraiment?
honour (*bill, commitments*) honorer
hope espérer
I hope that ... j'espère que ...
I hope so/not j'espère que oui/non
hors service *out of order*
hors taxes *non taxable, duty free*
hospital un hôpital
hospitality: **thank you for your hospitality**

merci de votre hospitalité
host l'hôte *m*
hostess l'hôtesse *f*
hot chaud(e)
they're selling like hot cakes ça se vend comme des petits pains
hotel un hôtel
at my hotel à mon hôtel
Hôtel de ville *Town Hall*
hour une heure
see also **time**
hourly (*rate*) horaire
house une maison
how comment
how many combien (de ...)
how much combien (de ...)
how long (*time*) combien de temps
how long/wide is it? quelle en est la longueur/largeur?
how often? (*precisely*) à quels intervalles?, avec quelle fréquence?
how often do you go there? est-ce que vous y allez souvent?
how long have you been with this company? depuis combien de temps est-ce que vous travaillez avec cette société?
how are you? comment allez-vous?
however cependant
however much we try ... nous avons beau essayer ...
HT hors taxes: *duty free*
hundredweight *1cwt=50.8 kilos*
hungry: **I'm hungry** j'ai faim
I'm not hungry je n'ai pas faim
hurry: **I'm in a hurry** je suis pressé(e)
please hurry! dépêchez-vous!
there's no hurry il n'y a pas d'urgence
if you can hurry things along si vous pouvez faire accélérer les choses

hurt: **it hurts** ça fait mal
husband: **my husband** mon mari
hypermarket un hypermarché
hypothèque *mortgage*
I: **I am** je suis
  I have j'ai
ice de la glace
  with lots of ice avec beaucoup de glace
ice-cream une glace
idea un idée
  good idea une bonne idée
  new ideas des idées nouvelles
  this will give you some idea of ... ça vous donnera une idée de ...
ideal idéal(e)
identical identique
idiot idiot(e)
i.e. c'est à dire
if si, **if not ...** sinon, ...
  if we could si nous pouvions
IFOP Institut Français d'Opinion Publique: *major opinion poll centre*
ill malade
  I feel ill je ne me sens pas bien
illegal illégal(e)
illegible illisible
image une image
  our company image l'image de marque de notre société
immediate immédiat(e)
  in the immediate future dans un futur immédiat
immediately immédiatement
immobilier *real estate*
immobilisations *fixed assets, permanent assets*
imperfect imparfait(e)

import importer
important: **it's very important** c'est très important
import duty un droit d'entrée
importer l'importateur *m*
import-export business l'import-export *m*
import licence une licence d'importation
import permit un permis d'importer
import restrictions des restrictions à l'importation
impossible impossible
impôts *tax, duties*
impressive impressionnant(e), remarquable
improve améliorer
an improved offer une offre supérieure
improvement: **we've made some improvements** nous avons apporté quelques améliorations
in dans
is he in? est-ce qu'il est là?
in Paris à Paris
in Scotland en Ecosse
in Canada au Canada
in 3 weeks' time dans trois semaines
we did it in 3 weeks nous l'avons fait en trois semaines
inch un pouce
» 1 inch=2.54 cm
incidental expenses les faux frais
include inclure
does that include breakfast? est-ce que le petit déjeûner est compris?
that's all included c'est tout compris
inclusive inclus(e)
are terms inclusive? est-ce que c'est tout compris?
income le revenu
incompetent incompétent(e)
inconvenient mal choisi(e), gênant(e)

incorrect inexact(e)
increase une augmentation
the increase in sales l'augmentation des ventes
in order to increase output afin d'augmenter le rendement
sales are increasing les ventes sont en hausse
at an increasing rate à un taux croissant
incredible incroyable
incur (*costs, expenses*) encourir
independent indépendant(e)
in-depth en profondeur, détaillé(e)
India l'Inde
Indian indien(ne)
indication une indication
as an indication of ... en signe de ..., pour vous montrer ...
indigestion une indigestion
indoors à l'intérieur
industrial industriel(e)
industrial action une action revendicative
industrial estate une zone industrielle
industrial relations les rapports entre syndicats et patronat
industry l'industrie
inexpensive bon marché
inferior inférieur(e)
inflation l'inflation *f*
influence l'influence *f*
inform renseigner
I am pleased to be able to inform you that je suis heureux de vous annoncer que
please inform us when ... veuillez nous faire savoir quand ...
keep me informed tenez-moi au courant

we'll keep you informed nous vous tiendrons au courant
you are very well informed vous êtes très bien informé
informal (*meeting*) sans façon, sans protocole (*agreement*) officieux(-euse)
information des renseignements
do you have any information in English about ...? est-ce que vous avez de la documentation en anglais sur ...?
for your information à titre de renseignement
initial (*an agreement*) parapher (*starting*) initial(e)
injured blessé(e)
innocent innocent(e)
input l'apport *m,* la fourniture
inscription *registration*
INSEE Institut National de la Statistique et des Etudes Economiques
inside à l'intérieur (de ...)
do you have inside information? est-ce vous avez des tuyaux?
insist: **I insist (on it)** j'y tiens absolument
inspect examiner, inspecter
inspector un inspecteur, un contrôleur
inspection une inspection, un contrôle
regular inspections des inspections régulières
closer inspection showed that ... une inspection plus poussée a montré que ...
installations des installations
instead à la place
instead of ... au lieu de ...
instruction: **delivery instructions** les instructions pour la livraison
as per your instructions suivant vos instructions
instructions for use le mode d'emploi

insurance un assurance
insurance claim la déclaration de sinistre
insurance company la compagnie d'assurance
insurance policy la police d'assurance
insurance premium la prime d'assurance
insure assurer
insured assuré(e)
  adequately insured against ... assuré correctement contre ...
insurmountable insurmontable
intelligent intelligent(e)
intend: we intend to ... nous avons l'intention de ...
  what do you intend to do? qu'est ce que vous avez l'intention de faire?
intensive intensif (-ive)
intention: it was our intention to ... nous avions l'intention de ...
interdit *prohibited*
interest l'intérêt *m*
  in the interests of speed pour des raisons de rapidité
  15% interest un intérêt de 15%
  interest rates les taux d'intérêt
  we are very interested in ... nous sommes très intéressés par ...
  are you interested in the idea? est-ce que cette idée vous intéresse?
interesting intéressant(e)
  we find it very interesting nous trouvons ça très intéressant
internal (*problems*) interne
international international(e)
interpret: would you interpret for us? pourriez-vous nous servir d'interprète?
interpreter un interprète

interruption une interruption
interview une entrevue
into dans
into France en France
into francs en francs
introduce: **can I introduce ...?** puis-je vous présenter ...?
invalid (*licence etc*) périmé(e)
inventaire *list; stocktaking*
invention une invention
invest investir
investment un investissement
investigate: **we'll investigate the matter** nous allons étudier la question, nous allons faire une enquête
investigations: **our investigations have shown that ...** nos recherches ont montré que ...
invisible invisible
invitation une invitation
thank you for the invitation merci de votre invitation
» *TRAVEL TIP: take a present such as flowers, chocolates or a cake, rather than a bottle of wine*
invite: **can I invite you out tonight?** puis-je vous inviter au restaurant ce soir?
invoice une facture
as per invoice selon notre facture
payable against invoice à payer à réception de la facture
within 30 days of invoice dans les trente jours après facturation
we'll invoice you direct nous facturerons directement
the amount invoiced le montant facturé
invoicing instructions les instructions de facturation
total annual invoicing la facturation annuelle totale

involve: **what does it involve?** qu'est-ce que cela comprend?, qu'est-ce que cela implique?
it would involve extra costs ça impliquerait des frais supplémentaires
we don't want to get involved in that nous ne voulons pas être impliqués là-dedans
IR impôt sur le revenu: *income tax*
Ireland l'Irlande
Irish irlandais(e)
iron: **will you iron this for me?** pouvez-vous me repasser ça?
iron out (*difficulties*) aplanir
is *see* **be**
isolated: **an isolated case** un cas isolé
issue (*of shares*) une émission
it: **it is** c'est; il (elle) est
put it there mettez-le(la) là
give it to him donnez-le(la) lui
it works ça marche
Italian italien(ne)
Italy Italie
item un article
all the items listed tous les articles inventoriés
itemize: **would you itemize it for me?** pouvez-vous me donner le détail?
an itemized invoice une facture détaillée
its *see* **my**
IUT Institut Universitaire de Technologie: *equivalent to Polytechnics*
jacket une veste
(*of book*) une jacquette
January: **in January** en janvier
Japan le Japon
Japanese japonais(e)
jealous jaloux(-ouse)

jeopardize compromettre
jet un jet [djet]
private jet un jet privé
jingle (*advertising*) un couplet publicitaire
jinx: **the project is jinxed** le sort s'acharne sur ce projet
JO Journal Officiel: *daily parliamentary bulletin listing new enactments*
job (*work*) un travail
(*position*) un poste
(*duty*) une fonction
just the job c'est juste ce qu'il nous faut
the job is yours vous êtes engagé!
it's a big job c'est une affaire importante
do you want the job? tenez-vous à ce poste/travail?
you've done a very good job vous avez fait du bon travail
what's your job? qu'est-ce que vous faites?
to offer somebody a job proposer un emploi à quelqu'un
that's your job c'est votre affaire
it's your job to get that done c'est à vous de vous en occuper
job description un profil de poste
job lot: **we'll take them as a job lot** nous les prenons au forfait
job-satisfaction la satisfaction au travail
joint commun(e)
joint venture une entreprise en association
joke une plaisanterie
you must be joking vous plaisantez!
journey un voyage
have a good journey bon voyage!
jours fériés *holidays*
jours ouvrables *week days*
judge: **judging by ...** à en juger par ...
July: **in July** en juillet
jump: **a sudden jump in sales** une brusque

hausse des ventes
we mustn't jump to conclusions il ne faut pas tirer des conclusions trop rapides
June: **in June** en juin
junk de la camelote
just: **just two** deux seulement
just a little un tout petit peu
just here/there ici/là
that's just right ça va très bien
not just now pas pour l'instant
just now maintenant
he was here just now il était là à l'instant
justifiable justifiable
justifiably avec raison
justify justifier
how can you justify that? comment pouvez-vous expliquer ça?
keel: **on an even keel** en équilibre
keen (*price, competition*) serré(e)
I'm not keen je n'y tiens pas tellement, ça ne me plaît pas beaucoup
keep: **can I keep it?** est-ce que je peux le garder?
you keep it gardez-le
keep the change gardez la monnaie
you didn't keep your promise vous n'avez pas tenu votre promesse
it keeps on breaking down il(elle) est tout le temps en panne
we'll keep on trying nous allons encore essayer
keep us informed tenez-nous au courant
key une clé
the key facts les faits déterminants
a key person une personne importante
he plays a key role il joue un rôle primordial
killing: **to make a killing** réussir un beau coup

kilo un kilo
» *conversion: kilos÷5×11=pounds*

kilos	*1*	*1½*	*5*	*6*	*7*	*8*	*9*
pounds	*2.2*	*3.3*	*11*	*13.2*	*15.4*	*17.6*	*19.8*

kilometre un kilomètre
» *conversion: kilometres÷8×5=miles*

kilometres	*1*	*5*	*10*	*20*	*50*	*100*
miles	*0.62*	*3.11*	*6.2*	*12.4*	*31*	*62*

kind: **that's very kind of you** c'est très aimable de votre part
would you be so kind as to ... auriez-vous la gentillesse de ...
if you would kindly send us ... si vous vouliez bien nous envoyer ...
knife un couteau
knockdown: **at a knockdown price** à un prix minimum
know savoir, (*be acquainted with*) connaître
I don't know je ne sais pas
do they know? est-ce qu'ils le savent?
I know him je le connais
do they know him? est-ce qu'ils le connaissent?
please let us know (what you decide) veuillez-nous faire savoir (ce que vous décidez)
I'll let you know je vous tiendrai au courant, je vous le ferai savoir
know-how le savoir-faire, le know-how
label une étiquette
labour (*personnel*) la main-d'oeuvre
(*work*) le travail
labour costs les frais de main-d'oeuvre
labour-intensive qui nécessite une main-d'oeuvre nombreuse
labour-saving qui allège le travail
lack: **there's a lack of ...** il y a pénurie de ...
ladies' les toilettes (des dames)
lady une dame
lager une bière

» *TRAVEL TIP: if you ask for 'une bière' you will automatically be served 'une bière blonde', which is lager-type beer*

land (*plane*) atterrir
language une langue
large grand(e)
  by and large d'une façon générale
last dernier(-ière)
  last year/week l'année/la semaine dernière
  last night hier soir
  at last! enfin!
  how long will this arrangement last? combien de temps est-ce que cet arrangement va durer?
late: **sorry I'm late** excusez-moi, je suis en retard
  please hurry, we are late dépêchez-vous, nous sommes en retard
  it's a bit late c'est un peu tard
later plus tard
  I'll come back later je reviendrai plus tard
  see you later! à tout à l'heure
  at the latest au plus tard
  latest development le dernier rebondissement, les faits nouveaux
latter: **the latter** le dernier, celui-ci
laugh rire
laughable ridicule
launch: **we are launching our new model** nous lançons notre nouveau modèle
launderette une laverie automatique
lavabos *toilets*
lavatory les toilettes *f*
law la loi
lawyer un juriste
  (*solicitor*) un avocat

layout (*of premises*) l'agencement *m*, la disposition, (*of report, text*) la présentation
lazy paresseux(-euse)
learn apprendre
lease louer (à bail)
(*contract*) un crédit-bail
leasing le leasing
leasing agent un agent de leasing
least: **not in the least** pas le moins de monde
at least au moins
leather le cuir
leave: **we're leaving tomorrow** nous partons demain
when does the plane leave? quand est-ce que l'avion part?
I left two shirts in my room j'ai laissé deux chemises dans ma chambre
can I leave this here? est-ce que je peux laisser ça ici?
I'll leave that up to you je vous laisse le soin de décider
let's leave that till later remettons ça à plus tard
left: **on the left** à gauche
left luggage (office) la consigne
leg la jambe
legal légal(e)
legal aid l'assistance judiciaire
we intend to take legal action nous avons l'intention d'engager des poursuites
legal costs les frais de justice
our legal advisor notre conseiller juridique
leisure: **at your leisure** à votre convenance
length la longueur
less moins (de ...)
less the costs of ... les coûts de ... en moins
let: **let us help** laissez-nous vous aider
will you let me off here? laissez-moi descendre ici

let's go allons-y
when can you let us have them? quand est-ce que vous nous les ferez parvenir?
we can't let that happen on ne peut pas laisser faire, il faut absolument éviter cela
letter une lettre
are there any letters for me? est-ce qu'il y a du courrier pour moi?
» *Start a letter with 'Monsieur' (or 'Madame', 'Mademoiselle') where you would have used 'Dear Sir', 'Dear Madam', and with 'Cher Monsieur' etc where you would have used 'Dear Mr Drew' etc. End the letter with 'Veuillez agréer, Monsieur, l'expression de mes sentiments distingués', or with 'Veuillez recevoir, cher Monsieur, l'assurance de mes meilleurs sentiments' (less formal)*
letterbox une boîte aux lettres
» *TRAVEL TIP: yellow, generally on walls*
letter of credit une lettre de crédit
to open a letter of credit émettre une lettre de crédit
level: **that will be decided at a higher level** la décision sera prise à un échelon supérieur
the current level of profits le niveau actuel des bénéfices
liabilities les dettes
(*on balance sheet*) le passif
liability: **we accept no liability for that** nous n'acceptons aucune responsabilité pour ça
liable (*responsible*) responsable
liaise with assurer la liaison avec
libre *vacant, free*
libre-service *self-service*
licence une licence
under licence sous licence

licensing agreement un accord de licence
lid un couvercle, un bouchon
lie (*falsehood*) un mensonge
  he's lying il ment
lieu de ... *place of ...*
  au lieu de ... *instead of ...*
life la vie
life assurance une assurance-vie
lift: **do you want a lift?** est-ce que je peux vous déposer quelque part?
  could you give me a lift? est-ce que vous pouvez me déposer quelque part?
  the lift isn't working l'ascenseur ne marche pas
light (*not heavy*) léger(-ère)
  the lights aren't working la lumière ne marche pas
  (*in car*) les phares ne marchent pas
  have you got a light? est-ce que vous avez du feu?
like: **would you like ...?** est-ce que vous voulez ...?
  I'd like a .../I'd like to ... j'aimerais ...
  I like it ça me plaît
  I don't like it ça ne me plaît pas
  like this one comme celui-ci
  what's it like? c'est comment?
  do it like this faites comme ça
limit: **up to a certain limit** jusqu'à une certaine limite
  a limited number of ... un nombre limité de ...
limite de validité *valid until ..., valid for ...*
limited company une société à responsabilité limitée
line une ligne
  what's their line of business? quel est leur secteur d'activité?
  a new line in ... une nouvelle gamme de ...
link une liaison

link up with établir des rapports avec
liqueur une liqueur
liquidation *clearance (sale)*
list une liste
it's not listed here ça ne figure pas sur la liste
listen écouter
listen! écoutez!
list price le prix de catalogue
literature (*brochures etc*) la documentation
litre un litre
» *1 litre=1¾pints=0.22 gals*

litres	*0.25*	*0.5*	*1*	*2*	*3*
pints	*0.44*	*0.87*	*1.75*	*3.5*	*5.25*

little petit(e)
a little ice un peu de glace
a little more un peu plus
just a little un tout petit peu
live: **I live in ...** j'habite à/en ...
where do you live? où est-ce que vous habitez?
livraison *delivery*
livret d'épargne *deposit*
load (*goods*) charger
each load chaque chargement
they will be loaded next Tuesday ils seront chargés mardi prochain
loan un prêt
local: **could we try a local wine?** est-ce qu'on pourrait essayer un vin de la région?
a local restaurant un restaurant du coin
a local call (*telephone*) une communication locale/urbaine
a local firm une entreprise locale
we use local labour nous employons la main-d'oeuvre locale
is it made locally? est-ce que c'est fabriqué

dans la région?
locataire *tenant*
location de voitures *car hire*
lock: the lock's broken la serrure est abîmée
I've locked myself out je me suis enfermé dehors
long long(longue)
I'd like to stay longer j'aimerais rester plus longtemps
that was long ago il y a longtemps de ça
how long? combien de temps?
there's a long way to go yet nous en sommes encore loin
long-term à long terme
in the long term à long terme, à longue échéance
look: can I have a look? est-ce que je peux jeter un coup d'oeil?
how do things look? comment ça se présente?
I'm looking for ... je cherche ...
I'm just looking je regarde
let's look at the report examinons le rapport
look at that regardez ça
look out! attention!
the figures look good les résultats paraissent satisfaisants
it looks tight ça a l'air juste
look forward: we look forward to meeting you again nous espérons vous revoir bientôt
loose (*goods*) en vrac
lorry un camion
lorry-driver un conducteur de camion
lose perdre
I've lost my ... j'ai perdu mon(ma) ...
excuse me, I'm lost excusez-moi, je me suis perdu
we're losing money nous perdons de l'argent
nobody loses out personne n'est perdant
loss une perte

we made a loss nous avons subi une perte
at a loss à perte
it's a loss-making concern c'est une entreprise qui travaille à perte
loss leader un article réclame (vendu à perte), un produit d'appel
lost property les objets trouvés
lot: **a lot (of ...)** beaucoup (de ...)
not a lot pas beaucoup
a lot of people/wine beaucoup de gens/vin
a lot more expensive (than ...) beaucoup plus cher (que ...)
loud fort(e)
louer: à louer *to let*
lovely très joli(e)
low (*level, returns*) faible
sales are at an all-time low les ventes sont à leur niveau le plus bas
low-key (*approach*) discret(-ète), sans emphase inutile
loyal loyal(e)
loyalty la loyauté
loyer *rent*
luck la chance, **bad luck** la malchance
good luck! bonne chance!
lucky: **you're lucky** vous avez de la chance
that's lucky c'est de la chance
luggage les bagages
lump sum un forfait, un montant forfaitaire
lunch le déjeuner
» *TRAVEL TIP: in Switzerland, 'déjeûner' is commonly used for breakfast, 'dîner' for lunch and 'souper' for dinner; the business lunch is somewhat of an institution, esp. in France*
Luxembourg le Luxembourg
luxury le luxe

---

au [oh], ç [s], ch [sh], e [uh, eh], é [ay], è [eh], eau [oh] -er [-ay], eu [er], -ez [-ay], gn [ny], i [ee], ou [oo], qu [k] y [ee]; *see also pp 4–5*

M. Monsieur: ***Mr***
machine une machine
mad fou(folle)
Madam Madame
magasin *shop, warehouse*
magazine un magazine
magnificent magnifique
mail le courrier
  is there any mail for me? est-ce qu'il y a du courrier pour moi?
mailing list un fichier d'adresses
mail order la vente par correspondance
mailshot un envoi de circulaires personnalisées
main principal(e)
  the main problem le problème essentiel
mainly principalement, essentiellement
maintenance contract un contrat d'entretien
Mairie *town hall*
major important(e)
  this is a major opportunity c'est une occasion importante
  the major points les points principaux
majority la majorité
majority holding une participation majoritaire
make faire
  will we make it in time? est-ce qu'on y arrivera à temps?
  what is it made of? en quoi c'est fabriqué?
  it's not making money ça ne rapporte pas
  I'll try to make him reconsider je vais lui demander de réexaminer sa décision
man un homme
management la gestion, l'administration *f*
  (*the managers etc*) la direction, les gestionnaires
  it's a question of good management c'est un problème de gestion
  our management are not in favour of ... notre direction n'est pas favorable à ...

manager un directeur, un chef de service
(*in hotel etc*) le gérant
production manager/sales manager/ publicity manager directeur de la fabrication/des ventes/de la publicité
manageress (*shop, restaurant*) la gérante
managing director le directeur général
man-hour une heure de travail
man management la gestion du personnel
manpower les effectifs
manual (*a book*) un manuel
(*operation*) manuel(le)
manufacture fabriquer
manufacturer un fabricant
many beaucoup (de ...)
map une carte
a map of Paris un plan de Paris
March: **in March** en mars
marchand de ... *dealer*
marchandises *goods*
Marché Commun *Common market*
margin la marge
marginal marginal(e)
mark une marque
market le marché
on the market sur le marché
we're not in the market for ... nous ne sommes pas intéressés par ...
to bring something onto the market mettre quelque chose en vente
what the market needs ce qu'on attend sur le marché, ce dont le marché a besoin
there's no market for it il n'y a aucun débouché pour ça
it was badly marketed ça a été mal lancé
it depends how you market it tout dépend

comment vous le lancez/commercialisez
the Money Market le marché monétaire
marketing le marketing
I'm in marketing je suis dans le marketing
our marketing policy notre politique commerciale
our marketing people nos commerciaux
we're very strong on marketing nous sommes très forts en marketing
marketing director le directeur du marketing
marketing manager le chef du service commercial
market leader le leader du marché, le numéro un du marché
market place: **in the market place** sur le marché
market research l'étude de marché
market trends les tendances du marché
mark-up une majoration, une marge
a 30% mark-up une majoration de 30%
marque *brand, make, trademark*
marque déposée *registered trademark*
married marié(e)
marvellous merveilleux(-euse)
masse salariale *aggregate remuneration to employees*
mass-produce fabriquer en série
match: **a box of matches** une boîte d'allumettes
material (*cloth*) du tissu
matières premières *raw materials, commodities*
matter: **it doesn't matter** ça ne fait rien
maturity (*of bill*) l'échéance *f*
maximize maximiser
maximum (le) maximum
that's our maximum offer c'est notre offre maximum
May: **in May** en mai
may: **may I have ...?** est-ce que je peux avoir ...?
maybe peut-être

Me Maître: *form of address for a barrister*
me: **does he know me?** est ce qu'il me connaît?
give it to me donnez-le moi
will you send it to me? pouvez-vous me l'envoyer?
with me avec moi
meal un repas
mean: **what does this mean?** qu'est-ce que ça veut dire?, **what do you mean?** qu'est-ce que vous voulez dire?
I mean it! je ne plaisante pas!
by all means bien entendu
meantime: **in the meantime** dans l'intervalle, entre temps
meet: **I met him last year** je l'ai rencontré l'année dernière
when do we meet again? quand est-ce que nous nous revoyons?
meeting (*conference*) une réunion, une assemblée, (*encounter*) une rencontre
at our last meeting lors de notre dernière rencontre/réunion
I think we need another meeting je crois qu'il nous faut prévoir une nouvelle réunion
member un membre
how do I become a member? comment est-ce que je peux devenir membre?
memo un mémo, une note
mention: **don't mention it!** je vous en prie!
as I mentioned in my letter ainsi que je le mentionnais dans ma lettre
menu la carte
set menu le plat du jour, un menu à prix fixe
can I have the menu, please? est-ce que je peux avoir la carte, s'il vous plaît?
see the menu reader, pp 104–107

Entrées/Crudités: Starters

Caviar *caviare*
Bouchées à la reine *chicken vol-au-vent*
Foie gras *liver pâté*
Confit d'oie *potted goose*
Terrine du Chef *pâté maison*
Fruits de mer *seafood platter*
Crudités variées *various salads and raw vegetables*
Cuisses de grenouille *frogs' legs*
Escargots *snails*
Quenelles *dumplings in sauce*
Salade de tomates/de céleri/d'endives/de concombres *tomato/celeriac/chicory/cucumber salad*
Salade verte *green salad with French dressing*
Salade de pommes de terre *potato salad*
Salade niçoise *salad with green beans, peppers, anchovies and olives*

Potages: Soups

Bouillon de poule *chicken consommé*
Potage printanier *spring vegetable soup*
Soupe à l'oignon *onion soup*
Velouté de tomate *cream of tomato*
Crème de bolets *cream of mushroom*
Soupe de poissons *fish soup*
Bisque d'écrevisses *crayfish bisque*

Viandes: Meat dishes

Boeuf *beef*, porc *pork*, veau *veal*, agneau *lamb*
Bifteck *steak*
Rôti de boeuf/porc *roast beef/pork*
Gigot d'agneau *shoulder of lamb*
Côtelette de porc *pork chop*
Escalope à la crème/panée *veal with cream/in breadcrumbs*

Langue de boeuf *tongue*
Foie de veau *calf's liver*
Tournedos *fillet steak*
Paupiettes de veau *veal olives*
Rognons madère *kidneys in madeira sauce*
Longe d'agneau *loin of lamb*
Pot au feu *beef stew*
Boeuf en daube *casserole of beef*

Volaille: Poultry
Poulet rôti *roast chicken*
Poulet Basquaise *chicken in wine and peppers sauce*
Canard à l'orange *duck with orange*
Poule au pot *chicken stew*
Coquelet à la crème *spring chicken with cream*
Cailles rôties *roast quails*

Gibier: Game
Civet de lièvre *jugged hare*
Gigue de chevreuil *haunch of venison*
Sanglier *wild boar*

Poissons et crustacés: Fish and seafood
Coquilles Saint-Jacques *scallops*
Vol au vent aux fruits de mer *seafood vol-au-vent*
Moules marinière *mussels in white wine*
Truite aux amandes *trout with almonds*
Raie au beurre noir *skate in black butter*
Filets de sole/perche *fillets of sole/perch*
Huîtres *oysters*
Loup au fenouil *bass with fennel*
Homard à l'armoricaine *lobster in white wine sauce with shallots*
Langouste *lobster*
Rouget au four/grillé *grilled mullet*
Sardines en friture *fried sardines*
Cabillaud au court-bouillon *poached cod*
Maquereaux au vin blanc *mackerel in white wine*

A few menu terms: à l'ail *(with) garlic*, aux câpres *in caper sauce*, à la crème *with cream*, échalotes *shallots*, garni *with chips (or rice) and vegetables*, en gelée *in aspic*, moutarde *mustard*, oignons *onions*, provençale *cooked in olive oil with garlic, tomatoes and herbs*, au vin blanc *in white wine*, vinaigrette *sharp oil and vinegar dressing*

Légumes: Vegetables

Pommes de terre dauphine *potato croquettes*
Pommes vapeur *steamed potatoes*
Pommes (de terre) frites *French fried potatoes*
Purée *mashed potatoes*
Haricots verts *French beans*
Gratin de courgettes *baby marrows 'au gratin'*
Carottes Vichy *baby carrots glazed with sugar and butter*
Endives braisées *braised chicory*
Epinards à la crème *creamed spinach*
Artichauts *artichoke*, asperges *asparagus*, champignons *mushrooms*, choux *cabbage*, choux de Bruxelles *Brussel sprouts*, choux-fleur *cauliflower*, fenouil *fennel*, tomates *tomatoes*

Fromages: le plateau de fromages *cheese board*

SOFT CHEESES

Brie, Camembert, Coulommiers, Munster, Reblochon, Vacherin

FIRM CHEESES

Roquefort, Bleu des Causses, Rigotte de chèvre, St. Marcellin, Gruyère, Comté

in Switzerland: mainly Gruyère, Emmenthal, fromage de Bagnes (Valais)

» *TRAVEL TIP: cheese, esp. in France, is an integral part of the meal and is served before dessert, generally with bread (not biscuits)*

Desserts

Glace *ice-cream*, crème chantilly *whipped cream*, compote *stewed fruit*, flan *egg custard*

Vacherin glacé *meringue cake with ice cream and fruit*

Tarte aux pommes/myrtilles *apple/bilberry tart*

Omelette norvégienne *baked Alaska*

Fruits de saison: cerises *cherries*, fraises *strawberries*, poires *pears*, pommes *apples*, pêches *peaches*, abricots *apricots*, raisin *grapes*, prunes *plums*

Snacks

Croque-monsieur *toasted ham and cheese sandwich*, Croque-madame *same as* croque-monsieur, *with egg*, Omelette au jambon/fromage *ham/cheese omelet*, Assiette anglaise, viande froide *cold meats*, Saucisses, frites *Frankfurter-type sausages with chips*, Sandwich au saucisson/jambon *salami-type/ham sandwich*, Crêpes *pancakes*, Oeufs sur le plat *fried eggs*

Spécialités

Aïoli *garlic mayonnaise*

Bouillabaisse *rich fish soup*

Choucroute garnie *sauerkraut with Frankfurter sausages, knuckle of ham etc*

Fondue bourguignonne *beef fondue: pieces of steak, dipped into hot oil and eaten with various sauces*

Fondue au fromage *cheese fondue: crusty pieces of bread dipped into melted cheese (usu. Gruyère)*

Raclette *(Switzerland) melted cheese served with boiled potatoes and pickles*

Viande séchée (or des Grisons) (*Switzerland*) *wafer-thin slices of cured beef, usu. served with rye bread and pickles*

Enjoy your meal! – or, as they say, **bon appétit!**

merchandise (*goods*) la marchandise
(*to market*) commercialiser
merchandising la commercialisation, le marchandisage
merger la fusion
mess: **the whole thing's a mess** c'est un désastre
message: **are there any messages for me?** est-ce qu'il y a un message/une commission pour moi?
can I leave a message for ...? est-ce que je peux laisser un mot pour ...?
messieurs *men, gents'*
metal le métal
method la méthode
metre un mètre
» *1 metre=39.37 ins=1.09 yds*

metres	*1*	*2*	*3*	*5*	*10*	*100*
feet	*3.3*	*6.6*	*10*	*16.6*	*33*	*333*

métro *underground*
» *TRAVEL TIP: flat fare on whole network of Paris métro; there are 1st class carriages (centre of train); a 'carnet de tickets' (book of tickets) is more economical than single tickets; tickets valid on Paris bus network, and on RER (Greater Paris express commuter train) within the city area*
microchip une 'puce', une plaquette de silicium miniaturisée
microcomputer un micro-ordinateur
mid: **by mid June** d'ici à la mi-juin
middle le milieu
by the middle of next month d'ici au milieu du mois prochain
in the middle au milieu
Middle East le Moyen-Orient
middleman un intermédiaire
middle management les cadres moyens
midnight minuit

might: **I might be wrong** j'ai peut-être tort
he might have gone il se peut qu'il soit parti
mile un mille
» *conversion: miles÷5×8=kilometres*

miles	*0.5*	*1*	*3*	*5*	*10*	*50*	*100*
kilometres	*0.8*	*1.6*	*4.8*	*8*	*16*	*80*	*160*

milk du lait
millimetre un millimètre
mind: **I've changed my mind** j'ai changé d'avis
I don't mind ça ne me dérange pas
do you mind if I ...? est-ce que ça vous dérange si ...?
please bear this in mind ne l'oubliez pas
his/my mind is made up il a/j'ai décidé
I'm sure they won't mind je suis sûr que ça ne les dérangera pas
never mind tant pis
mine *see* **my**
mineral water de l'eau minérale
minimize réduire au minimum
minimum (le) minimum
minor (*problems*) mineur(e), secondaire
minus moins
minute une minute
(*tiny*) minuscule
he'll be here in a minute il sera là dans un instant
just a minute un petit instant, je vous prie
minutes: **to take the minutes of a meeting** rédiger le compte rendu d'une réunion, rédiger le procès-verbal d'une réunion
misgivings: **I have misgivings** j'ai des doutes
Miss Mlle, Mademoiselle
miss: **there's a ... missing** il y a un(une) ... qui manque
if we miss the deadline si nous dépassons la

date limite
I don't want to miss my plane je ne veux pas manquer mon avion
mistake une erreur
I think you've made a mistake je crois que vous vous êtes trompé
misunderstand: **don't misunderstand me** comprenez-moi bien
misunderstanding un malentendu
mix mélanger
(*mixture*) un mélange
a good mix of products une bonne variété de produits
mix-up un malentendu
Mlle Mademoiselle: *Miss*
MM. Messieurs: *Messrs*
Mme Madame: *Mrs*
Mo. Métro: *underground*
mobile mobile
mobilier *(of) stock, (of) securities*
mode d'emploi *directions for use*
model un modèle
modern moderne
modernize moderniser
modification une modification
moins *less, minus*
moment un moment
at the moment en ce moment
Monday lundi
money: **I've lost my money** j'ai perdu mon argent
I have no money je n'ai pas d'argent
» *TRAVEL TIP: the unit in French currency is 'un franc', divided up into 100 'centimes'; main coins are 10 centimes, 20c, 50c, 1F, 2F, 5F and 10F; the 10F coin is easily mistaken for coins of lesser value (no 10Fr. coin in Switzerland); main notes are 10F, 20F, 50F, 100F, 500F*
money order un mandat-poste

monitor (*results*) contrôler
monopoly le monopole
montant *amount, sum total*
month un mois
monthly mensuel(le)
(*occurring*) chaque mois, tous les mois
more plus (de ...)
can I have some more? est-ce que je peux en avoir plus?, **more wine, please** encore du vin, s'il vous plaît
there isn't/aren't any more il n'y en a plus
there aren't any more ... il n'y a plus de ...
no more c'est tout, ça suffit
more comfortable plus confortable
more than 10 plus de dix
morning le matin
this morning ce matin
good morning bonjour (Monsieur *etc*)
in the morning le matin
most: **I like it most** c'est celui que je préfère
most of the time/most of the people la plupart du temps/des gens
motivated motivé(e)
motor le moteur
motorway l'autoroute *f*
» *TRAVEL TIP: toll motorways in France (relatively expensive), but free in Switzerland; you either pay at the 'péage' (toll-station) or get a card there and pay on exit; most M-ways are 2-lane only; be extra careful where lanes merge*
move: **could you move your car?** est-ce que vous pouvez déplacer votre voiture?
he's moved to another department/company il a changé de service/de société
we've moved nous avons déménagé
he's the man to get things moving c'est

l'homme qu'il faut pour faire progresser les choses
Mr M., Monsieur
Mrs, Ms Mme, Madame
much beaucoup (de ...)
much better/much more beaucoup mieux/ plus, **not much** pas beaucoup
multinational (*company*) une multinationale
must: **I must have ...** je dois avoir ..., il faut que j'aie ..., (*supposition*) je dois avoir ...
I must not eat ... je ne dois pas manger de ...
we must do it nous devons le faire, il faut que nous le fassions
you must not ... vous ne devez pas ...
that's a must c'est une nécessité
mutual: **in our mutual interests** pour nos intérêts réciproques, dans l'intérêt de nos deux sociétés, **to our mutual satisfaction** à la satisfaction de chacun
my: my, your *etc*; **mine, yours** *etc*:

	singular	*plural*
my	mon (ma)	mes
your	votre	vos
informally	ton(ta)	tes
his, her, its	son (sa)	ses
our	notre	nos
their	leur	leurs

his/her car sa voiture
his/her umbrella son parapluie
» *'son' etc before a feminine noun starting with vowel:* son automobile
mine le mien (la mienne), les miens (les miennes)
yours le (la) vôtre, les vôtres, *informally* le tien (la tienne), les tiens (les tiennes)
his, hers le sien (la sienne), les siens (les siennes)
ours le (la) nôtre, les nôtres
theirs le (la) leur, les leurs

name un nom
my name is ... je m'appelle ...
what's your name? quel est votre nom?
what's his name? comment s'appelle-t-il?
napkin une serviette
narrow étroit(e)
national national(e)
he's a Swiss national il est de nationalité suisse
nationality la nationalité
nationalize nationaliser
natural naturel(le)
near: is it near? est-ce que c'est près d'ici?
near here près d'ici
do you go near ...? est-ce que vous passez près de ...?
where's the nearest ...? où est le(la) ... le(la) plus proche?
nearly presque
neat (*drink*) sec
necessary nécessaire
as necessary selon les besoins
if necessary s'il le faut, si besoin est
it's not necessary ce n'est pas nécessaire
necessitate nécessiter
necessity une nécessité
need: I need a ... j'ai besoin d'un ..., il me faut un ...
we need more time nous avons besoin de plus de temps, il nous faut plus de temps
the need for ... le besoin de ...
negative négatif(-ive)
a negative response une réaction négative
negligent négligent(e)
negotiable négociable
not negotiable non négociable

negotiate: **to negotiate a settlement** négocier un règlement
we are currently negotiating with ... nous sommes actuellement en pourparlers avec ...
negotiations les négociations
negotiator un négociateur(une négociatrice)
neither: **neither of them** aucun des deux
neither ... nor ... ni ... ni ...
neither do I moi non plus
net net(te)
net price un prix net
£5000 net cinq mille livres net
net of tax taxes déduites
the net margin la marge nette
nettoyage à sec *dry-cleaning*
network (*of distributors etc*) un réseau
never jamais
new nouveau(-elle), (*not used*) neuf (neuve)
I'm new to the job je débute dans ce travail
news (*press*) les nouvelles
what news do you have about developments in ...? que savez-vous sur ce qui se passe en/dans ...
newspaper un journal
newspaper article un article de journal
do you have any English newspapers? avez-vous des journaux anglais?
in the newspaper dans le journal
New Zealand la Nouvelle Zélande
next prochain(e)
please stop at the next corner arrêtez-vous au prochain croisement
see you next week à la semaine prochaine
on my next trip lors de mon prochain voyage
at the next opportunity à la prochaine occasion
next we have to ... ensuite, nous avons à ...
next to ... à côté de ...
nice joli(e)

night la nuit
good night bonne nuit
at night la nuit
where's a good night club? où est-ce qu'il y a un bon night club?
night-life la vie nocturne
night-porter le portier de nuit
no non
no improvement pas d'amélioration
no change pas de changement
no extras pas de suppléments
no way! pas question!
No. n°
nobody personne
nobody is buying them personne n'en veut, personne ne les achète
noisy bruyant(e)
our room's too noisy notre chambre est trop bruyante
nombre *number*
non-committal: **he was non-committal** il ne s'est pas engagé
non-delivery la non-livraison
non-dutiable non taxable, exempté des droits de douane
non-fulfilment la non-exécution
non-fumeurs *non smokers*
non-productive improductif(-ive)
non-starter: **this idea is a non-starter** ceci n'entre même pas en ligne de compte
none: **none of them** aucun d'entre eux
nonsense des absurdités
nonsense! c'est ridicule!
normal normal(e)
when things are back to normal quand les choses seront revenues à la normale

---

normally normalement
north le nord
Northern Ireland l'Irlande du Nord
Norway la Norvège
Norwegian norvégien(ne)
not: **I'm not hungry** je n'ai pas faim
not that one pas celui-ci
not me pas moi
I don't understand je ne comprends pas
he didn't tell me il ne m'a pas dit
notary un notaire
note (*bank note*) un billet (de banque)
I'll make a note of it j'en prendrai note
my notes of the meeting mes notes de réunion
we note your ... nous prenons note de votre ...
please note that ... veuillez noter que ...
see **credit, dispatch** *etc*
nothing rien
nothing new rien de nouveau
I heard nothing je n'ai rien entendu
notice (*on notice-board*) un avis
I didn't notice that je n'ai pas remarqué ça
until further notice jusqu'à nouvel ordre
it has come to our notice that ... nous avons remarqué que ...
we should like to bring the following to your notice ... nous aimerions porter à votre connaissance ...
we need more notice than that nous avons besoin d'être prévenus plus tôt
how much advance notice do you need? combien de temps à l'avance voulez-vous être prévenu?
without any notice sans avertissement préalable
I have handed in my notice j'ai donné ma démission
notify: **we will notify you when ...** nous vous

ferons savoir quand ..., nous vous aviserons quand ...
please notify us veuillez nous en aviser
notorious notoire
November: **in November** en novembre
now maintenant
nowhere nulle part
nuisance: **it's a nuisance** c'est ennuyeux
null and void nul et non avenu
number (*figure*) un nombre
a number of problems un certain nombre de problèmes
number 57 numéro 57
which number? quel numéro?
numéro de commande *order number*
numéro de compte *account number*
object (*item*) un objet
do you object? est-ce que ça vous ennuie?, est-ce que vous y voyez un inconvénient?
I object to that je ne suis pas d'accord avec ça
objection une objection
I've no objections je n'ai rien à redire
would you have any objections if ...? est-ce que vous verriez un inconvénient à ce que ...?
objective (*goal*) un objectif
(*unbiased*) objectif(-ive)
objets trouvés *lost property (office)*
obligataire *(of) debentures*
obligation *bond, debenture*
obligation: **without obligation** sans obligation
obligatory obligatoire
obliged: **we would be very much obliged if you ...** nous vous serions obligés de bien vouloir ...
obliging obligeant(e)
oblique: **'2 oblique 4'** deux-barre-quatre

obsolete périmé(e)
obstacle un obstacle
obtain (*get*) obtenir
obvious évident(e)
obviously ... bien entendu ...
obviously not! bien sûr que non!
occasion: **on the next occasion** à la prochaine occasion
if the occasion should arise si l'occasion devait se présenter
occasionally de temps en temps
occupation (*job*) l'occupation *f*, l'emploi *f*
occupé *engaged, taken*
occupied occupé(e)
is this seat occupied? est-ce que cette place est prise?
occur se produire
o'clock *see* **time**
October: **in October** en octobre
odd (*strange*) étrange
odd number un nombre impair
of de
off: **10% off** 10% de réduction
£3 off avec une réduction de trois livres
the meeting is off la réunion est annulée
the deal is off l'affaire est à l'eau
offer: **we accept your offer** nous acceptons votre offre
I'll make you an offer je vais vous faire une proposition
a special offer une offre spéciale
what sort of conditions are you offering? qu'est-ce que vous offrez comme conditions?
they only offered 10% ils n'ont offert que 10%
office le bureau
office supplies les fournitures de bureau
office automation la bureautique
official (*person*) un responsable
the official version la version officielle

in my official capacity dans l'exercice de mes fonctions
off-load décharger
offre spéciale *special offer*
often souvent
oil (*petroleum*) le pétrole
(*lubricating –, vegetable – etc*) l'huile *f*
OK d'accord
old vieux(vieille)
how old is he? quel âge a-t-il?
old-fashioned démodé(e)
omit omettre
OMS Organisation Mondiale de la Santé: *WHO*
on: **on the table** sur la table
I haven't got it on me je ne l'ai pas sur moi
on Friday vendredi
on television à la télévision
the deal is on again l'affaire est repartie
OK, you're on d'accord, j'accepte
the engine is on le moteur est en marche
the light is on la lumière est allumée
once une fois
at once tout de suite
once it is signed dès signature, une fois que ce sera signé
one: **number** un(une)
the red one le(la) rouge
one-off: **a one-off operation/order** une opération/commande isolée
we'll do this one as a one-off il nous faudra le faire spécialement
only seulement
this is the only one c'est le(la) seul(e)
ONU Organisation des Nations Unies: *UNO*
OP Ouvrier Professionnel: *skilled worker*
OPA Offre Publique d'Achat: *takeover bid*

---

open ouvert(e), (*verb*) ouvrir
when do you open? quand est-ce que vous ouvrez?
to open an account ouvrir un compte
to open a new branch ouvrir une nouvelle succursale
open-ended (*agreement*) sans limites fixes
OPEP Organisation des Pays Exportateurs de Pétrole: *OPEC*
operate (*machine*) faire fonctionner
the area of business in which we operate le secteur dans lequel nous travaillons
operating capital le capital d'exploitation
operating costs (*of a business*) les frais d'exploitation
operation: **our overseas operations** nos activités à l'étranger
when we put this new system into operation quand nous avons mis ce nouveau système en service
operator (*telephone*) une téléphoniste, une standardiste
(*machine*) un opérateur(une opératrice)
» *TRAVEL TIP: in France, dial 10 to call the operator*
opinion une opinion
in our opinion à notre avis
what's your opinion? qu'en pensez-vous?
opportunity une occasion
I was glad to have the opportunity of ... j'ai été heureux d'avoir l'occasion de ...
opposite: **opposite the hotel** en face de l'hôtel
option une option
if you'd like an option on the next model si vous voulez une option sur le prochain modèle
we have no option nous n'avons pas le choix
or ou
orange (*colour*) orange
order (*for goods*) une commande

(*a command*) un ordre
(*goods, dish*) commander
could we order now? (*in restaurant*) est-ce que nous pourrions commander maintenant?
thank you, we've already ordered merci, nous avons déjà commandé
if we place an order with you for ... si nous vous commandons ..., si nous vous passons commande de ...
the last order hasn't arrived la dernière commande n'est pas arrivée
we have a very full order book notre carnet de commandes est très chargé
the parts are still on order les pièces détachées sont encore en commande
the goods we ordered les marchandises que nous avons commandées
in order to ... afin de ...
order form un bulletin de commande
order number le numéro de la commande
ordinary ordinaire
ordinary shares des actions ordinaires
organization: **good/poor organization** une bonne/mauvaise organisation
organize organiser
origin: **country of origin** le pays d'origine
original original(e)
the original ... le premier(la première) ...
do you have the original? est-ce que vous avez l'original?
originally à l'origine
ORTF Office de la Radio et Télévision Françaises: *French Broadcasting Authority*
OS Ouvrier Spécialisé: *unskilled worker*
OTAN Organisation Traité Atlantique Nord: *NATO*

other autre
the other one l'autre
do you have any others? est-ce que vous en avez d'autres?
otherwise autrement
ought: **it ought to be here by now** il(elle) devrait être là, maintenant
ounce une once
» *1 ounce=28.35 grammes*
our, ours *see* **my**
out dehors
that's 5% out il y a un écart/une erreur de 5%
9 out of 10 neuf sur dix
is he still out? est-ce qu'il n'est toujours pas rentré?
outlet (*retail*) un point de vente
we need new outlets (*markets*) il nous faut de nouveaux débouchés
outline: the broad outlines (*of the proposal*) les lignes générales (de notre proposition)
output le rendement, la production
outside dehors
outside the EEC à l'extérieur du Marché Commun
outside advisors des experts-conseils indépendants
outstanding (*invoice, payment*) impayé(e)
£5000 is still outstanding il y a un arriéré de cinq mille livres
ouvert *open*
ouvrir: ne pas ouvrir *do not open*
over: **over here** ici
over there là-bas
over 40 plus de quarante
it's all over c'est fini
over a period of 6 months sur une période de six mois
overcome (*difficulties*) surmonter
overdraft un découvert

overdraft facility des facilités de caisse
overdrawn à découvert
overdue (*payment*) en souffrance, en retard
overheads les frais généraux
overnight: **an overnight stay in Dijon** une nuit (passée) à Dijon
will we have to stay overnight? est-ce qu'il faut prévoir une nuit à l'hôtel?, est-ce que nous y passerons la nuit?
overnight travel is necessary il faudra voyager de nuit
overpriced: **it's overpriced** le prix est trop élevé, le prix est surfait
overseas à l'étranger, outremer
overseas sales les ventes à l'exportation
oversleep: **I overslept** je ne me suis pas réveillé à temps
overstock un excédent de stock
overtime les heures supplémentaires
owe: **what do we owe you?** combien est-ce que nous vous devons?
money owing to us l'argent qui nous est dû
owing to ... en raison de ...
own: **my own ...** mon(ma) propre ...
I'm on my own je suis seul(e)
owner le propriétaire
pack un paquet
package l'emballage *m*
(*set of services etc*): **we have an attractive package** nous avons une formule (globale) intéressante
you have to take the whole package il vous faut prendre le tout ensemble
attractively packaged conditionné de façon attrayante
packaging (*material*) l'emballage *m*

packet un paquet
packing l'emballage *m*
packing case une caisse
packing instructions les instructions pour l'emballage
packing list la liste de colisage
page (*of book*) une page
  could you page him? est-ce que vous pourriez le faire appeler?
paiement à la commande/livraison *CWO/COD*
pain: **I've got a pain here/in my leg** j'ai mal ici/à la jambe
  pain-killers des calmants *m*
pair une paire
Pakistan le Pakistan
Pakistani (*person*) un Pakistanais(une Pakistanaise)
pale pâle
pallet une palette
paper le papier
  (*newspaper*) un journal
papers (*documents*) les documents
par: par retour de courrier *by return of post*
  par route/mer *by road/sea*
parcel un paquet, un colis
parcmètre *parking meter*
pardon (*didn't understand*) pardon?
  I beg your pardon (*sorry*) excusez-moi
parent company la maison-mère
park: **where can I park my car?** où est-ce que je peux garer ma voiture?
part *share (of ...)*
part une partie
  (*of machine*) une pièce
  part consignment une expédition partielle
  part load un chargement partiel
  part owner un copropriétaire
  part payment un acompte
participation *interest (stock held), profit-*

sharing, contribution
particular particulier(ière)
in particular en particulier
particulars (*specifications etc*) des renseignements, des détails
particulier vend ... *for private sale ...*
partner un associé(une associée)
partnership une association
parts *shares (stock)*
party (*group*) un groupe
(*celebration*) une réunion (entre amis), une petite fête
(*to contract*) une partie
both parties are agreed that ... les parties en cause ont convenu que ...
pass on (*information*) transmettre
I'll pass it on to him je vais le lui faire savoir
passage interdit *no entry*
passage protégé *stretch of main road where traffic coming from the side roads doesn't have right of way*
passif *liabilities, 'capital (or funds) employed'*
passport un passeport
past: **in the past** autrefois
patent un brevet
we have applied for the patent nous avons déposé la demande de brevet
patient: **be patient** soyez patient(e)
pattern (*on material*) un dessin, un motif
pay payer
how shall we pay you? comment voulez-vous être payé?
to pay the money back rembourser
can I pay, please? est-ce que je peux payer, s'il vous plaît?
payable payable

payé *paid*
payee le bénéficiare
payer le payeur
payment le paiement
payment will be made in 3 instalments le paiement se fera en trois versements
method of payment les modalités de paiement
conditions of payment les conditions de paiement
monthly payments of ... des versements mensuels de ...
we are still awaiting payment of ... nous attendons toujours le paiement de ...
pcc. pour copie conforme
PCV communication en PCV: *reverse charge call*
PDG Président-Directeur Général: *chairman and managing director*
peak (*of figures, production*) un maximum
pedestrian crossing un passage pour piétons
» *TRAVEL TIP: do not assume that cars will stop or even slow down once you are on a pedestrian crossing, be extra cautious*
pen: **have you got a pen?** est-ce que vous avez un stylo?
penalty clause une clause pénale
pencil un crayon
pension une pension
(*OAP's*) une pension de retraite, une retraite
pension scheme une formule de retraite
people les gens
will there be a lot of people there? est-ce qu'il y aura beaucoup de monde?
a lot of people think that ... beaucoup de gens pensent que ...
if people like the product si le produit plaît (au public)
per: **per night/week/person** par nuit/semaine/personne

as per instructions suivant les instructions
as per contract selon le contrat
per cent pour cent
percentage le pourcentage
a fixed percentage un pourcentage fixe
on a percentage basis au pourcentage
percepteur *tax collector*
perfect parfait(e)
performance (*of machine, worker etc*) le rendement
(*of company*) les résultats *m*
perhaps peut-être
period une période
périphérique *'le périphérique' is the Paris ring road*
permanent permanent(e)
permis *permit, licence*
permission une autorisation
permit un permis
person une personne
in person en personne
personal personnel(le)
personally personnellement
personne physique *private individual*
personne morale *legal entity*
personnel le personnel
personnel department le service du personnel
personnel manager le chef du personnel
persuade: we want to persuade you to ... nous voulons vous persuader de ...
perte *loss*
petrol de l'essence
petrol station une station-service
YOU MAY SEE OR HEAR ... ...
super=*4-star*
ordinaire, normale=*2-star*

---

au [oh], ç [s], ch [sh], e [uh, eh], é [ay], è [eh], eau [oh] -er [-ay], eu [er], -ez [-ay], gn [ny], i [ee], ou [oo], qu [k] y [ee]; *see also pp 4–5*

le plein? *do you want it filled up?*
» *TRAVEL TIP: the pump attendant will expect a tip if he gives your windscreen a wipe; routine checks such as 'les niveaux' (oil and battery level) can be costly*
pharmacie de garde *chemist's on duty*
phase une phase
phase in introduire progressivement
phase out supprimer graduellement
phone *see* **telephone**
photograph un photo
picture une photo
(*print, drawing etc*) une image
(*painting*) un tableau
piece: **a piece of ...** un morceau de ...
pièces jointes *enclosures*
piétons *pedestrians*
pin down: **we must try and pin him down to a date** il faut que nous arrivions à lui faire préciser une date
pint *approx.* un demi-litre *(1 pint=0.57 litre)*
» *TRAVEL TIP: if you ask for a beer, the standard measure is 33 cl, slightly more than a half-pint*
pipe (*metal*) un tuyau
(*smoker's*) une pipe
pity: **it's a pity** c'est dommage
PJ – Ann Pièces jointes – annexes: *enclosures*
place un endroit
at my/your place? chez moi/vous?
is this place taken? est-ce que cette place est prise?
the meeting will take place in London la réunion aura lieu à Londres
to place an order with somebody passer commande à quelqu'un
placements *investment(s)*
plain (*food*) simple
(*not patterned*) uni(e)
plan un plan

according to plan selon les prévisions
plans of the building les plans de construction
we are planning to ... nous projetons de ...
still at the planning stage encore à l'état de projet
plane un avion, **by plane** en avion
plant (*factory*) une usine
(*equipment*) l'équipement, les installations
plastic le plastique
platform le quai
which platform please? c'est à quel quai?
pleasant agréable
please: **could you please ...?** s'il vous plaît, est-ce que vous pouvez ...?
(yes) please oui, s'il vous plaît
pleased: **we are pleased with ...** nous sommes contents de ...
pleased to meet you enchanté(e)
pleasure: **it's a pleasure** avec plaisir
my pleasure! je vous en prie!
plenty: **plenty of ...** beaucoup de ...
thank you, that's plenty merci, ça suffit
plug une prise (électrique)
plus plus
plus-value *appreciation*
PLV Publicité au Lieu de Vente: *point of sale promotion*
p.m. *see* **time**
PME Petites et Moyennes Entreprises: *small and medium-sized businesses*
PMI Petites et Moyennes Industries: *small and medium-sized industries*
PMU Pari Mutuel Urbain: *state-controlled betting (horse-racing)*
PNB Produit National Brut: *GNP*

pocket une poche
poids lourds *heavy goods vehicles*
point le point
four point six quatre virgule six
there are three points to be discussed il y a trois points à discuter
that's a very important point c'est un point essentiel
point 16 on the list la rubrique 16 de la liste
we'd like to draw your attention to the following points nous aimerions attirer votre attention sur les points suivants
he has a point son argument est valable
from our/ your point of view de notre/votre point de vue
could you point to it? pouvez-vous l'indiquer?
point of sale un point de vente
at point of sale au point de vente
point of sale material la matériel de publicité au point de vente
police la police
get the police appelez la police
policeman un agent de police
police station le commissariat
policy (*of company*) la politique, la ligne de conduite
(*insurance*) la police (d'assurance)
polish (*shoes*) du cirage
could you polish my shoes? pouvez-vous cirer mes chaussures?
polite poli(e)
politics la politique
poll (*opinion-*) un sondage
polluted pollué(e)
polythene bag un sac en plastique
pompiers *fire brigade*
pool (*swimming*) une piscine
poor pauvre
poor quality une qualité médiocre

Portugal le Portugal
Portuguese portugais(e)
popular apprécié(e) du public
  a very popular line une gamme très appréciée
port payé carriage paid
port dû carriage forward
portefeuille portfolio, investments
porter (*at station etc*) un porteur
position une position
  I'm not in a position to say je ne suis pas en mesure de le dire
positive positif(-ive)
  a positive response une réaction positive
porteur: au porteur to bearer
possession: **the goods will be in your possession** vous recevrez les marchandises
possibility la possibilité
possible possible
  a possible development might be ... une conséquence éventuelle serait ...
  as ... as possible aussi ... que possible
  could you possibly ...? est-ce que vous pourriez ...?
post (*job*) un poste, un emploi
  it'll be in the post tomorrow ça partira au courrier de demain
  I'll have it posted to you je vous le ferai envoyer
postage l'affranchissement
postage rates le tarif postal
postcard une carte postale
poste item (on account)
poste restante poste restante
poster une affiche
post office un bureau de poste

postpone ajourner, remettre
potential potentiel(le)
  it has a lot of potential ça offre des possibilités intéressantes
pound une livre
» *conversion: pounds÷11×5=kilos*

pounds	*1*	*3*	*5*	*6*	*7*	*8*	*9*	*11*
kilos	*0.45*	*1.4*	*2.3*	*2.7*	*3.2*	*3.6*	*4.1*	*5*

NB: a French pound=500 grammes
pour *for*
pourboire *tip*
poussez *push*
power: **purchasing power** le pouvoir d'achat
précautions avant usage *handle with care*
practical pratique
precedent précédent(e)
prefer: **I prefer this one** je préfère celui-ci
  I'd prefer to ... j'aimerais mieux ...
  I'd prefer a ... je préfèrerais un(une)
premises les locaux
  on the premises sur place
premium une prime
  premium offer une offre spéciale
present: **at present** en ce moment
presentation (*of new product*) la présentation
president le président
press: **could you press these?** est-ce que vous pouvez repasser ces vêtements?
  the Press la presse
pressure: **you'll have to put more pressure on them** il faudra que vous fassiez pression sur eux
  he's under a lot of pressure il est sollicité de toutes parts
prestation *service, cover, performance*
prêt *loan*
pre-tax avant impôt
pretty joli(e)
  it's pretty good c'est pas mal du tout

previous précédent(e)
at our previous meeting lors de notre réunion précédente
the previous agreement l'accord précédent, l'accord antérieur
price un prix
your prices are very reasonable/high vos prix sont très raisonnables/élevés
price list le tarif
pricing policy la politique des prix
pricing structure la structure des prix
prime *premium*
principal (*of order*) le mandant
(*of investment, debt*) le capital
print (*verb*) imprimer
(*of negative*) une épreuve
(*reproduction etc*) une illustration
we enclose a colour print of ... veuillez trouver ci-joint une illustration couleur de ...
printed matter des imprimés
printer (*person*) un imprimeur
(*machine*) une imprimante
print-out un listing
prior: **I have a prior engagement** j'ai un engagement antérieur
priorité (à droite) *right of way (to vehicles coming from the right)*
priority la priorité
it's not a priority ce n'est pas prioritaire
in order of priority par ordre de priorité
will you treat this as a priority? pouvez-vous considérer ceci comme prioritaire?
private privé(e)
a private discussion un entretien privé
a private meeting une réunion privée
a private company une société à

responsabilité limitée
privatize privatiser
prix de revient *cost price*
prix de vente *retail price, selling price*
prix d'achat *purchase price*
probably probablement
probably not c'est peu probable
problem un problème
no problem c'est sans problème
procedure la procédure, la marche à suivre
proceedings: **we shall take proceedings against you/them** nous intenterons contre vous/eux une action en justice, nous vous/les poursuivrons en justice
process un processus, une opération
it's being processed right now on s'en occupe en ce moment
procès-verbal *minutes; (parking etc) ticket*
procuration *proxy, power of attorney*
produce (*verb*) fabriquer, produire
product un produit
production la production
we start production on ... nous commençons la production le ...
production manager le directeur de la production
produits *products; proceeds, profits*
professional: **it's a very professional piece of work** c'est du travail de professionnel
not a very professional approach une méthode pas très professionnelle
profit le profit, le bénéfice
profit margin la marge bénéficiaire
profit and loss account le compte de résultats
profitability la rentabilité
profitable rentable
profit-sharing l'intéressement *m*, la participation aux bénéfices
pro-forma invoice une facture pro forma

programme (*plan*) un programme
progress: **we are making good progress** nous progressons de façon satisfaisante
  what progress have you made? quels progrès avez-vous fait?
project un projet
promise: **do you promise?** est-ce que vous le promettez?
  I promise je promets, d'accord
promissory note un billet à ordre
promote (*product*) promouvoir
  (*employee*) donner de l'avancement à
  it's been well/badly promoted ça a été bien/mal lancé, la promotion a été bien/mal faite
promotion (*of product*) la promotion
  for promotion purposes à des fins de promotion, pour la promotion
pronounce: **how do you pronounce it?** comment est-ce que ça se prononce?
properly correctement
property la propriété
proposal une offre, une proposition
propriétaire *owner*
prospectus *leaflet, folder*
protect protéger
proud fier(fière)
  we are proud of our record nous sommes fiers de nos résultats/réalisations
prove: **I can prove it** je peux le prouver
provide fournir
  we'll provide you with ... nous vous fournirons ...
provided ... à condition que ...
provisional (*temporary*) provisoire
provisionally provisoirement
provisions *reserves*

proviso une condition
Pte *on Paris map:* Porte
PTT, P & T Postes et Télécommunications: *the Post Office*
public: **the public** le public
to create more public awareness focaliser l'attention du public
to monitor the public's reaction suivre de près la réaction du public
public company une société anonyme
to go public émettre des actions publiques
public holiday un jour férié
» *TRAVEL TIP: public holidays are:*
New Year's Day *le Nouvel An*
Good Friday *Vendredi-Saint*
Easter Monday *le lundi de Pâques*
May Day *le premier mai*
Ascension Day *l'Ascension*
Whit Monday *le lundi de Pentecôte*
Christmas Day *Noël*
there is also:
l'armistice (8 mai–1945)
la fête nationale (le 14 juillet)
l'assomption (15 août)
la Toussaint (premier novembre)
l'armistice (11 novembre–1918)
and in Switzerland:
la fête nationale (le premier août)
publicity la publicité
publicity budget le budget publicitaire
publicity campaign la campagne de publicité
publicity manager le chef de la publicité
publicity material le matériel publicitaire
pull tirer
punctual ponctuel(le)
puncture une crevaison
purchase (*noun*) un achat
(*verb*) acheter
purchase order un bon de commande

pure pur(e)
purple violet(te)
purpose le but, l'intention *f*
  on purpose exprès
purse un porte-monnaie
push pousser
  we want to push this line hard nous voulons mettre l'accent sur la promotion de cette gamme
put: **where can I put ...?** où est-ce que je peux mettre ...?
  where have you put it? où est-ce que vous l'avez mis?
  where do I put it? où est-ce que je le mets?
  we want to put the deadline back nous aimerions repousser la date limite
PV Procès-Verbal: *(parking/speeding etc) ticket*
QG Quartier Général: *HQ*
quai *quay, platform*
  à quai *ex quay*
qualified: **I'm not qualified to comment** je ne suis pas qualifié pour donner mon avis
qualified acceptance une acceptation assortie de conditions, une acceptation conditionnelle
qualitative qualitatif(-ive)
quality la qualité
quality control le contrôle de la qualité
quality control department le service contrôle qualité
quantitative quantitatif(-ive)
quantity: **what sort of quality do you envisage?** quelle quantité envisagez-vous?
quarter (*3 months*) un trimestre, trois mois
  quarterly trimestriel(le)
  (*done, occuring*) tous les trois mois, chaque trimestre

a quarter of an hour un quart d'heure
see also **time**
query une question
question une question
do you have any other questions? avez-vous d'autres questions?
questionnaire un questionnaire
queue la queue, la file d'attente
» *TRAVEL TIP: don't necessarily expect orderly queuing*
quick rapide
that was quick ça a été rapide
quiet: **a quiet time of the year** une période calme de l'année
quite assez
quite a lot beaucoup
quittance *receipt*
quota le quota, le contingent
quotation, quote un devis
(*binding*) une cotation
quote: **we'd like to quote for ...** nous aimerons vous fournir une cotation pour ...
at the price we quoted au prix fixé
quote-part *share (of ...)*
r. rue: *street*
rabais *discount, rebate*
radio la radio
rail: **by rail** en train
(*send goods*) par train
rain la pluie
it's raining il pleut
raincoat un imperméable
raise: **to raise finance** se procurer des fonds, trouver des capitaux
to raise the interest rate augmenter le taux d'intérêt
range (*of products*) une gamme
a new range une nouvelle gamme
rappel *on traffic signs: reminder*

rare rare
(*steak*) saignant(e)
rate: **the rate of exchange** le taux de change, le cours du change
our rates for this year nos tarifs pour cette année
the rate of increase/growth le taux de croissance
at a monthly rate of 2% à un taux mensuel de 2%
at any rate quoi qu'il en soit, de toute façon
rather: **I'd rather have a ...** je préférerais un(une) ...
I'd rather not j'aimerais mieux pas
it's rather expensive c'est plutôt cher
RATP Régie Autonome des Transports Parisiens: *the Paris transport authority*
raw materials les matières premières
razor un rasoir
razor blades des lames de rasoir
reach (*agreement*) arriver à, aboutir à
read: **read it** lisez-le
something to read quelque chose à lire
ready: **when will it be ready?** quand est-ce que ce sera prêt?
real (*genuine*) véritable
the real cost le coût réel
réalisable *cashable; feasible*
really vraiment
reason une raison
there are several reasons why ... il y a plusieurs raisons au fait que ..., ... pour plusieurs raisons
reasonable raisonnable
receipt un reçu, une quittance
(*in restaurant etc*) une note

can I have a receipt, please? est-ce que je peux avoir une quittance?
we are in receipt of ... nous avons reçu ...
please acknowledge receipt (of ...) veuillez accuser réception de ...
on receipt of ... dès réception de ...
recently récemment
récépissé *receipt*
reception la réception
at reception à la réception
receptionist le(la) réceptionniste
receive (*goods, order*) recevoir
recession la récession
réclamation *complaint*
recognize reconnaître
recommend: **can you recommend ...?** pouvez-vous recommander ...?
recommandé *registered*
reconsider: **we are willing to reconsider** nous sommes prêts à réexaminer
record un record
in record time en un temps record
a record level un niveau record
this is strictly off the record ceci est strictement confidentiel
please keep a record of ... veuillez noter ... n'oubliez pas de noter ...
they have an excellent record leurs résultats passés sont excellents
reçu *receipt*
red rouge
the company's in the red la société est en déficit
we are now out of the red nous ne sommes plus en déficit
reduce diminuer, réduire
reduction une diminution, une réduction
réduction *discount*
refer: **we refer to your recent letter** nous nous

référons à votre lettre récente
reference: **with reference to ...** en référence à ...
our/your reference nos/vos références
reference number la référence
refuse: **I refuse** je refuse
they are refusing to pay ils refusent de payer
regard: **with regard to ...** en ce qui concerne ..., pour ce qui est de ...
regarding your inquiry en ce qui concerne votre demande
as regards price/quality en ce qui concerne le prix/la qualité
region une région
in this region dans cette région
in the region of £5000 aux environs de cinq mille livres
registered: **I want to send it registered** je voudrais l'envoyer en recommandé
règlement *settlement; regulations*
règlement judiciaire *liquidation, receivership*
regret: **I very much regret that ...** je regrette beaucoup de/que ...
we regret what has happened nous regrettons ce qui est arrivé
regular régulier(-ière)
regulations le règlement
relation: **the relations between our two companies** les relations entre nos deux sociétés
in the interests of good relations dans l'intérêt de nos relations, afin de favoriser de bonnes relations
relationship les relations
relevant: **the relevant ...** le(la) ... approprié(e)
that's not relevant ça n'a pas de rapport, ça

n'a rien à voir (avec ...)
relevé *statement*
reliable (*product*) fiable
they are reliable on peut compter sur eux, on peut leur faire confiance
rely: **you can rely on it** vous pouvez compter dessus
remaining: **the remaining work** le travail restant, le travail qui reste (à faire)
remember: **don't you remember?** vous ne vous souvenez pas?, vous ne vous rappelez pas?
I'll always remember je m'en souviendrai toujours
if I remember rightly ... si je me souviens bien ...
remind: **we would remind you that ...** nous aimerions vous rappeler que ...
reminder un rappel
final reminder un dernier rappel
remise *allowance, discount*
renew (*contract etc*) renouveler
renseignements *information*
rent: **can I rent a car?** est-ce que je peux louer une voiture?
YOU MAY THEN HEAR ...
un forfait kilométrique *mileage charge*
repair: **can you repair it?** est-ce que vous pouvez le(la) réparer?
repeat: **could you repeat that?** est-ce que vous pouvez répéter?
repeat order une commande renouvelée
replace replacer
reply (*noun*) une réponse
(*verb*) répondre
in reply to ... en réponse à ...
report (*noun*) un rapport
our annual report notre rapport de gestion annuel
we shall report back to you nous vous

présenterons un rapport
who does he report to? quel est son supérieur hiérarchique?
report à nouveau *balance carried forward, 'profit retained'*
representative un représentant
reprocess recycler
reputation la réputation
request (*noun*) une demande
(*verb*) demander
on request sur demande
requirements: **we hope this meets your requirements** nous espérons que ceci répondra à vos besoins
our present stock requirements nos besoins actuels de stocks
RER Réseau Express Régional: *Greater Paris express commuter network; one of the best ways into Paris from Charles-de-Gaulle airport: take the 'navette' (shuttle bus) to the 'gare SNCF/RER', then direct to 'Gare du Nord'*
rescue sauver
research la recherche
research and development department le service de recherche et développement
reservation une réservation
I want to make a reservation for ... (*hotel*) je voudrais faire une réservation pour ...
(*theatre*) je voudrais réserver une place pour ...
reserve: **can I reserve a seat/table?** est-ce que je peux réserver une place/table?
we reserve the right to ... nous nous réservons le droit de ...
see also **book**
réserve légale *statutory reserves*
resign: **he's resigned** il a donné sa démission

responsibility: **this is your responsibility** c'est à vous de vous en occuper
we cannot accept responsibility nous déclinons toute responsabilité
responsible responsable
rest le reste
you keep the rest vous pouvez garder le reste
restaurant un restaurant
result: **as a result of this** en conséquence
the year's results les résultats de l'année écoulée
excellent results des résultats excellents
retailer un détaillant
retail outlet un point de vente (au détail)
retail price le prix de détail
retired à la retraite
return: **a return (ticket) to ...** un aller-retour pour ...
by return of post par retour de courrier
by return of telex par télex retour
the returns on this investment la rentabilité de cet investissement
if the returns are satisfactory si les rentrées sont satisfaisantes
we are returning the substandard specimens nous vous renvoyons les exemplaires de qualité inférieure
réunion *meeting*
revenu *income*
reverse charge call une communication en PCV
revise (*plan*) réviser
rez-de-chaussée *ground floor*
RF République Française
rich riche
ridiculous ridicule
right: **you don't have the right to ...** vous n'avez pas le droit de ...
that's right c'est juste

you're right vous avez raison
on the right à droite
right here ici même
rights les droits
we keep all the rights nous réservons tous droits
if we grant you the manufacturing rights si nous vous cédons les droits de fabrication
rights issue une émission prioritaire
rip off: **it's a rip-off** c'est du vol organisé
rise (*in prices, costs*) une augmentation
ristourne *cash discount*
riverains *local residents*
RN Route Nationale: *trunk road, A road*
road une route
which is the road to ...? quelle est la route pour ...?
rob: **I've been robbed** on m'a dévalisé(e)
room une chambre
there isn't enough room il n'y a pas assez de place
have you got a (single/double) room? est-ce que vous avez une chambre (pour une personne/deux personnes)?
for one night/for three nights pour une nuit/ trois nuits
YOU MAY THEN HEAR ...
avec ou sans salle de bains? *with or without bath?*
avec douche? *with shower?*
pour combien de personnes? *for how many people?*
pour combien de temps? *for how long?*
désolé, c'est complet *sorry, full up*
room service le service des chambres
roughly approximativement

roulez lentement *go slow*
round: **in round figures** en chiffres ronds
to round a figure up arrondir un chiffre
it's my round c'est ma tournée!
route un itinéraire
please specify delivery route veuillez indiquer l'itinéraire pour la livraison
by the usual sea route par la route maritime habituelle
routier: relais routier *transport café*
» *TRAVEL TIP: 'relais routiers' are good and relatively inexpensive restaurants; don't hesitate to try them: look for the red and blue circular sign*
royalty les droits d'auteur
rubber du caoutchouc
rubberband un élastique
rubbish les déchets
rubbish! quelle blague!, c'est ridicule!
rubrique *item, heading*
rude impoli(e)
rum du rhum
rum and coke un rhum coca
run: **a run on the market** une demande soudaine, une montée soudaine de la demande
running costs (*for organization*) les frais d'exploitation
Russia la Russie
Russian russe
SA Société Anonyme: *limited company*
sad triste
we are sad to hear that ... nous sommes désolés d'apprendre que ...
safe (*strong box*) un coffre(-fort)
(*operation*) sans danger
is it safe? est-ce qu'il y a des risques?
safety la sécurité
salary un salaire
sale la vente

they're not for sale ils ne sont pas à vendre
on a sale or return basis à condition
sales les ventes
sales are improving/dropping off les ventes progressent/diminuent
volume of sales le volume des ventes
total sales for the past year le total des ventes pour l'année écoulée
sales campaign une campagne de vente
sales department le service des ventes
sales director le directeur des ventes
sales drive une campagne de ventes, une relance des ventes
sales manager le responsable des ventes
salesman un vendeur
you're a good salesman vous êtes un bon vendeur, vous êtes doué pour la vente
sales-orientated: **a more sales-orientated approach** une approche plus orientée vers la vente
sales outlet un point de vente
sales target un objectif de vente
saleswoman une vendeuse
salle d'attente *waiting room*
salle à manger *dining room*
same: **the same** le(la) même, (*plural*) les mêmes
the same again please! la même chose, s'il vous plaît!
sample un échantillon
the sample models les échantillons
not up to sample non conforme à l' échantillon
SARL Société à responsabilité limitée: *limited company*
satisfaction: **to our/your complete satisfaction** à notre/votre entière satisfaction

satisfactory satisfaisant(e)
a very satisfactory solution une solution très satisfaisante
your performance is not satisfactory vos résultats ne sont pas satisfaisants
satisfy: **we are not satisfied with ...** nous ne sommes pas satisfaits de ...
I hope you will be satisfied with ... nous espérons que vous serez satisfait de ...
we are not satisfied that everything possible has been done nous ne sommes pas convaincus que tout ait été fait
Saturday samedi
save: **this way we save £5000** de cette façon nous économisons cinq mille livres
it saves a lot of bother cela épargne bien des ennuis
in order to save time afin de gagner du temps
saving: **a considerable saving in costs/time** une économie considérable de frais/de temps
say: **how do you say ... in French?** comment est-ce qu'on dit ... en français?
what did he say? qu'est-ce qu'il a dit?
what do you say to that? qu'en pensez-vous?
do we have a say in ...? est-ce que nous avons notre mot à dire en ce qui concerne ...?
schedule un programme
on schedule conforme aux prévisions (*train etc*) à l'heure
we are on schedule nous sommes dans les temps
we are ahead of schedule nous sommes en avance sur le programme
behind schedule en retard
scheduled for ... prévu pour ...
scheduled flight un vol régulier
scissors: **a pair of scissors** une paire de ciseaux
scope (*of project etc*) l'étendue *f*, le champ
that's beyond the scope of these talks cela

sort du cadre de ces discussions
Scot un Ecossais(une Ecossaise)
Scotland l'Ecosse
Scottish écossais(e)
screen un écran
sea la mer
by sea par mer
sea freight le fret maritime
season une saison
in the high/low season en haute/basse saison
seat une place
is this somebody's seat? est-ce que cette place est occupée?
seat belt une ceinture de sécurité
second (*2nd*) deuxième, second(e)
(*time*) une seconde
just a second un instant, s'il vous plaît
second class en seconde
second hand d'occasion
seconds (*goods*) des articles de qualité inférieure
secretary une secrétaire
(*company secretary*) le secrétaire général
sector: **in the private/public sector** dans le secteur privé/public
secure (*an order*) assurer
(*a loan*) garantir
security (*for loan*) une caution
(*of premises etc*) la sécurité
see voir
oh, I see je comprends, je vois
have you seen ...? est-ce que vous avez vu ...?
can I see the samples? est-ce que je peux voir les échantillons?
I'd like to see your figures j'aimerais voir vos chiffres

---

see you tomorrow/next week à demain/la semaine prochaine
seem: **it seems ...** cela semble ...
it seems so il semble bien
seldom rare
selection (*of goods*) un choix
self-financing autofinancé(e)
self-service (*shop*) un libre-service
(*restaurant*) un self-service
sell vendre
to sell something to somebody vendre quelque chose à quelqu'un
if you can sell them the idea si vous pouvez les en convaincre
they are selling well/slowly ils se vendent bien/lentement
send envoyer
I'll send one to you je vais vous en envoyer un
would you send us some samples? pourriez-vous nous envoyer quelques échantillons?
the goods are to be sent by container les marchandises seront envoyées/expédiées par conteneur
send it by post envoyez-le(la) par la poste
sender l'expéditeur *m*
sens unique *'one way'*
separate: **under separate cover** sous pli séparé
that's a separate matter c'est une autre question
it's a separate company c'est une société indépendante
separately séparément
September: **in September** en septembre
serial number un numéro de série
series une série
(*line of products*) une collection
a new series une nouvelle collection
serious sérieux(-euse)
I'm serious je ne plaisante pas

this is serious c'est grave
service: **is service included?** est-ce que le service est compris?
we're not satisfied with the service we're getting nous ne sommes pas satisfaits du service clients
we are pleased to be of service to you nous sommes heureux de vous être utiles
his service to the company sa contribution à la marche de la société
it's all part of the service cela fait partie du service
service industries le secteur tertiaire
service station une station service
servicing contract un contrat d'entretien
servicing manual un manuel d'entretien
set (*adjust*) régler
a set of new parts un jeu/assortiment de pièces de rechange
let's set a date fixons une date
settle: **I want to settle this before I leave** j'aimerais régler ça avant de partir
please settle your account veuillez régler votre facture
please settle within 30 days veuillez régler dans les trente jours
settlement: **a satisfactory settlement** un règlement satisfaisant
in settlement of our account en règlement de notre compte
we look forward to receiving your settlement dans l'attente de votre règlement
settlement discount une remise
set up (*company*) constituer
several plusieurs
SGDG Sans Garantie Du Gouvernement: *not*

officially approved by French Standards body
shake secouer
to shake hands with ... serrer la main à ...
let's shake on it! scellons le marché!
» *TRAVEL TIP: shaking hands is common on meeting and leaving somebody*
shame: **what a shame** quel dommage!
shampoo un shampooing
shandy une bière panachée
» *TRAVEL TIP: likely to be lager and lemonade*
shape la forme
shape up: **it's shaping up well** ça prend forme, c'est en bonne voie
share une part
(*equity*) une action
(*verb*) partager
we must share the blame nous en partageons la responsabilité
share-capital le capital actions
share-holder un actionnaire
sharp practice des procédés malhonnêtes
shaver un rasoir
shaving foam de la mousse à raser
she elle
sheet of paper une feuille (de papier)
shelf une étagère
sherry un xérès
ship un bateau
(*send*) expédier
by ship par bateau
the goods will be shipped to you next week les marchandises vous seront expédiées la semaine prochaine
shipment: **the next shipment of ...** la prochaine expédition de ...
they will be ready for shipment on ... ils seront prêts à l'expédition le ...
each shipment chaque envoi
shipping agent l'agent maritime

shipping documents les documents maritimes
shipping instructions les instructions pour l'expédition
shirt une chemise
shock un choc
shoes des chaussures
shop un magasin
I've some shopping to do j'ai des courses à faire
shop steward un délégué syndical
short court(e)
at short notice à bref délai
I'm three short il m'en manque trois
in the short term à court terme
short cut un raccourci
shortage: **a shortage of ...** une pénurie de ...
shortfall (*in figures, supplies*) un déficit
show: **the items on show** les articles exposés
please show me ... veuillez me montrer ...
we were shown round the factory on nous a fait visiter l'usine
showcase une vitrine
shower: **with shower** avec douche
showroom le magasin d'exposition
shrink-wrapped emballé (à chaud) sous film plastique
shut fermer, (*closed*) fermé(e)
when do you shut? quand est-ce que vous fermez?
SICAV Société d'Investissement à Capital Variable: *unit trust*
sick malade
I feel sick je ne me sens pas bien
side le côté, **on this side** de ce côté
he does that on the side il fait ça à côté
we're on your side nous sommes à vos côtés,

nous sommes avec vous
side street une rue adjacente
by the side of the road au bord de la route
sight: **payable on sight** payable à vue
three days after sight à trois jours de vue
when we have sight of your order dès réception de votre commande
sight bill une traite à vue
sign (*notice*) un écriteau
please sign here veuillez signer ici
to sign a contract signer un contrat
it's not signed ce n'est pas signé
I'm not signing that! je ne signerai pas ça!
signature une signature
silly stupide
silver l'argent *m*
similar semblable
simple simple
since: **since last week** depuis la semaine dernière
since they want to get started now puisqu'ils veulent commencer maintenant
sincere sincère
yours sincerely meilleures salutations; *see also* **letter**
single: **single room** une chambre pour une personne
I'm single je suis célibataire
a single/two singles to ... un aller/deux aller pour ...
sit: **can I sit here?** est-ce que je peux m'asseoir ici?
site: **a good/pleasant site** un bon emplacement
situation la situation
the financial/economic situation la situation financière/économique
in the present situation dans la conjoncture actuelle
a cut-back situation une situation de

récession
situation *position*
size la taille, les dimensions
skill le talent, le savoir-faire
skilled worker un ouvrier professionnel
skirt une jupe
sleep: **I can't sleep** je ne peux pas dormir
sleeper (*train*) un wagon-lit
sleeping pill un somnifère
slide (*photo*) une diapositive
slide presentation une présentation de diapos
sliding scale une échelle mobile
slow lent(e)
that's too slow c'est trop lent
you're slowing down vous ralentissez
could you speak a little slower? est-ce que vous pouvez parler un peu plus lentement?
small petit(e)
small change de la petite monnaie
smell l'odeur *f*
SMIC Salaire Minimum Interprofessionel de Croissance: *minimum guaranteed wage*
SMIG Salaire Minimum Interprofessionel Garanti: *now superseded by the SMIC*
smoke la fumée
do you smoke? est-ce que vous fumez?
can I smoke? est-ce que je peux fumer?
» *TRAVEL TIP: smoking is prohibited in France in public buildings and on public transport, as well as in cinemas*
smooth lisse
please try to smooth things over essayez d'arranger les choses
it all went very smoothly cela s'est très bien passé
snack un snack, un casse-croûte

SNCF Société Nationale des Chemins de Fer Français: *the French Railways*
snow la neige
so: **so expensive** si cher
not so much pas tant
so so comme ci, comme ça
soap du savon
sober: **he wasn't sober** il avait bu
social: **it's a social visit** je ne viens pas pour affaires
social security la sécurité sociale
société *company*
soda (water) de l'eau de Seltz
SOFRES Société Française d'Enquêtes pour le Sondage: *opinion poll body*
soft drink une boisson sans alcool
soft sell une publicité discrète, une technique de vente en douceur
software le logiciel
soins d'urgence *emergencies, first aid*
solde *balance*
soldes *sale*
sole: **sole agency** l'exclusivité *f*
sole agent un agent exclusif
sole rights les droits exclusifs
solution une solution
some: **can I have some water/pepper?** pourriez-vous m'apporter de l'eau/du poivre?
can I have some cigars? pourriez-vous m'apporter des cigares?
can I have some? est-ce que je peux en avoir?
can I have some more? est-ce que je peux en avoir encore?
can I have some leaflets? est-ce que je peux avoir quelques dépliants?
some people think that ... certains estiment que ...
somebody quelqu'un
something quelque chose

sometime à un moment ou à un autre, à l'occasion
sometimes quelquefois
somewhere quelque part
somme *sum*
sondage *opinion poll, survey*
sonnez et entrez *please ring and enter*
soon bientôt
  as soon as possible dès que possible
sooner plus tôt
sore: **I have a sore throat** j'ai mal à la gorge
sorry: **I'm sorry** excusez-moi
  we are sorry to hear... nous sommes désolés d'apprendre ...
sort: **this sort** cette sorte
  what sort of ...? quelle sorte de ...?
  could you sort these out? pourriez-vous les trier?
  will you sort it out? pouvez-vous arranger ça?
sortie de secours *emergency exit*
soumission *tender*
sound: **it sounds interesting** ça a l'air intéressant
south le sud
South Africa l'Afrique du Sud
South America l'Amérique du Sud
souvenir un souvenir
space: **should there be extra space in the container** s'il y a de la place en plus dans le conteneur, s'il reste de la place dans le conteneur
  for reasons of space pour des raisons de place
Spain l'Espagne
Spanish espagnol(e)
spare: **spare part** une pièce détachée, une pièce de rechange

speak: **do you speak English?** est-ce que vous parlez anglais?
I don't speak French je ne parle pas français
special spécial(e)
special terms des conditions spéciales
special case un cas particulier
specialist un spécialiste, un expert
specialize: **we specialize in ...** nous sommes spécialisés dans ...
specially surtout, particulièrement
specific spécifique, particulier(-ière)
specifications spécifications
specify spécifier, indiquer
please specify time and place veuillez spécifier l'heure et l'endroit
please specify whether ... veuillez indiquer si ...
the items specified in our order les articles spécifiés dans notre commande
at the specified time/place à l'heure indiquée/à l'endroit indiqué
spectacles des lunettes
speed la vitesse
please speed things up veuillez activer les choses
spell: **how do you spell it?** comment ça s'écrit?
spend (*money*) dépenser
spirits des spiritueux, des alcools
split (*costs etc*) fractionner, partager
spoon une cuillère
spot: **our man on the spot** notre correspondant sur place
sprain: **I've sprained my ankle** je me suis foulé la cheville
spring un ressort
(*season*) le printemps
square (*in town*) une place
(*not circular*) carré(e)
2 square metres deux mètres carrés

staff le personnel
stage: **the next stage** l'étape suivante, le stade suivant
at this stage in the negotiations au point où en sont les négociations
stage *training session/period*
staggered payments des paiements échelonnés
stagnation la stagnation, le marasme
stairs les escaliers
stalls: **2 stalls** deux places d'orchestre
stamp un timbre
two stamps for England deux timbres pour l'Angleterre
» *TRAVEL TIP: in France you can buy stamps from many newsagents and some cafés; look for the sign 'tabac-journaux' or 'tabac'*
stand (*at fair*) un stand
we stand by what we said nous nous en tenons à ce que nous avons dit
standard standard
(*norm*) une norme, un critère
the standard of work is not satisfactory la qualité du travail n'est pas satisfaisante
British standards les normes britanniques
stand-by (*ticket*) un billet 'stand-by'
standing order un ordre de virement permanent
star une étoile
a three/four/five-star hotel un hôtel à trois/quatre/cinq étoiles, un hôtel de troisième/deuxième/première catégorie
start commencer
at the start au commencement
my car won't start ma voiture ne démarre pas
when does it start? ça commence quand?

starting next month à partir du mois prochain
statement (*bank* –) un relevé de compte
(*from supplier etc*) un relevé de factures
to make a statement on ... faire un communiqué sur ...
statement of account un relevé de compte
station la gare
bus station la gare routière
stationnement interdit *no parking*
stationnement limité à *restricted parking ...*
stay: **we enjoyed our stay** nous avons fait un très bon séjour
I'm staying at the Ritz/a friend's je séjourne au Ritz/chez un ami, je suis au Ritz/chez un ami
Sté Société: *company*
steady (*increase, improvement*) régulier(-ière), constant(e)
steak un steak
YOU MAY HEAR ...
à point *medium*
bien cuit *well done*
saignant *rare*
steep (*prices*) excessif(-ive)
steps: **what steps are you taking?** quelles mesures prendrez-vous?
we'll take the necessary steps nous prendrons les mesures nécessaires
sterling: **in sterling** en livres sterling
sticking plaster du sparadrap
still: **is he still here?** est-ce qu'il est encore là?
we're still waiting for them nous les attendons toujours
they're still the best ils restent les meilleurs
stock le stock
stocks are running low les stocks s'épuisent
they're out of stock ils ne l'ont plus en stock
our current stock position notre niveau de

stocks actuel
we don't stock them any more nous ne les avons plus en stock, nous ne les tenons plus
stock control la gestion des stocks
stock level l'état des stocks
Stock Exchange la Bourse
stockist le stockiste
stock list l'inventaire
stolen: **my wallet's been stolen** on m'a volé mon portefeuille
stomach: **I've got stomach-ache** j'ai mal au ventre
have you got something for an upset stomach? est-ce que vous avez quelque chose pour les maux de ventre?
stone la pierre
» *weight: 1 stone=6.35 kg*
stop: **we intend to stop supplies unless ...** nous avons l'intention d'arrêter la livraison à moins que ...
please stop all work arrêtez la production
do you stop near ...? est-ce que vous vous arrêtez près de ...?
stop-over une escale
stoppage un arrêt de travail
store (*shop*) un magasin
(*goods*) entreposer
storm une tempête
straight droit(e)
go straight on continuez tout droit
let's get things straight mettons les choses au point
we've always been straight with you nous avons toujours été francs avec vous
straight away immédiatement
straight whisky un whisky sec

strange étrange
stranger: **I'm a stranger here** je ne suis pas d'ici
strategy la stratégie
streamlined (*hull etc*) aérodynamique
a more streamlined operation une production rationalisée
street une rue
stress: **he's suffering from stress** il est stressé, il souffre de tension nerveuse
I want to stress the importance of ... j'aimerais souligner l'importance de ...
strike une grève
stringent strict(e)
strong fort(e)
a strong pound/dollar une livre forte/un dollar fort
study: **I want to study the figures** je voudrais étudier les chiffres
stupid stupide
style le style
subcontract: **if you subcontract the work to ...** si vous donnez le travail en sous-traitance à ...
subcontractor un sous-traitant
subject to ... sous réserve de ..., sujet à ...
submit: **to submit a report** soumettre un rapport
subscriber un abonné(une abonnée)
subscription un abonnement
to take out a subscription to ... prendre un abonnement à ...
subsidiary une filiale
subvention *grant, subsidy*
succeed réussir
if you succeed in improving sales si vous réussissez à améliorer les ventes
success le succès
I wish you every success je vous souhaite

sincèrement de réussir
successful (*trip*) réussi(e)
a successful business une affaire qui marche très bien
succursale branch
such: **such a lot** tellement
in such a hurry si rapidement
suddenly subitement
sue poursuivre en justice
we intend to sue nous avons l'intention d'intenter un procès
to sue for £50,000 réclamer cinquante mille livres de dédommagement en justice
suffer: **sales have suffered** les ventes ont souffert
sugar du sucre
suit (*man's*) un complet
(*woman's*) un tailleur
suitable approprié(e)
is that suitable? est-ce que ça vous convient?
not suitable for ... qui ne convient pas à ...
suitcase une valise
sum une somme
summary un résumé
summer l'été
sun le soleil
Sunday dimanche
supermarket un supermarché
supersede: **the model has been superseded by ...** ce modèle a été remplacé par ...
supplier: **our suppliers** nos fournisseurs
supply fournir
supply and demand l'offre et la demande
continuity of supply la régularité de l'approvisionnement
it's a supply problem c'est un problème

d'approvisionnement
our supplies are running out nos réserves s'épuisent
a new source of supply une nouvelle source d'approvisionnement
can you supply us with ...? pouvez-vous nous fournir ...?
we can supply them at 20% discount nous pouvons les fournir avec 20% de réduction
the various services/products which we can supply les différents services/produits que nous pouvons offrir
support: **we need your support** nous avons besoin de votre soutien
sur *on, out of*
sure: **I'm not sure** je ne suis pas sûr
are you sure? êtes-vous sûr?
I'm sure you will like them je suis sûr qu'ils vous plairont
please make sure that ... vérifiez s'il vous plaît que ...
surname le nom de famille
survey (*of market*) une enquête de marché
(*of property*) une expertise
suspend (*order*) suspendre
SVP s'il vous plaît: *please*
Sweden la Suède
Swedish suédois(e)
Swiss suisse
(*person*) un Suisse(une Suissesse)
switch un interrupteur
to switch on/off allumer/éteindre
Switzerland la Suisse
YOU MAY HEAR ...
la Suisse romande *French-speaking Switzerland*
la Suisse allemande *German-speaking Switzerland*
symbol le symbole

sympathetic: **we are very sympathetic with your position** nous comprenons fort bien votre position
syndic de faillite *receiver*
syndicat d'initiative *tourist office*
tabac-journaux *newsagent*
table une table
a table for 4 une table pour quatre
table wine un vin de table, un vin ordinaire
tailor: **tailored to your requirements** conçu(e) en fonction de vos besoins
take prendre
can I take this with me? est-ce que je peux emporter ça?
we'll take a thousand of each nous en prendrons mille de chaque
will you take them back? est-ce que vous les rapporterez?
will you take me to the airport? est-ce que vous pouvez m'emmener à l'aéroport?
it will take 3 months ça prendra trois mois
the plane takes off at ... l'avion part à ...
to take out an insurance policy contracter une assurance
I'll take you up on that je m'en souviendrai, je vous prends au mot
takeover un rachat, un prise de contrôle
takeover bid une offre publique d'achat, une O.P.A.
talk parler
talks les entretiens *m*
tantièmes *(directors') percentage of profits*
tape une bande magnétique
tape-recorder un magnétophone
target un objectif
we're on target nous sommes dans les

objectifs, nous respectons le programme
we're behind target nous ne faisons pas le programme, nous sommes en retard sur le programme
target date la date visée
target market le créneau visé, le marché visé
tariff un tarif
taste le goût, **it tastes horrible/very nice** c'est mauvais/délicieux
taux de l'intérêt *rate of interest*
tax: **tax returns** la déclaration d'impôts
before tax avant impôt, brut(e)
after tax après impôt, net(te)
taxable imposable
taxi un taxi
will you get me a taxi? est-ce que vous pouvez m'appeler un taxi?
where can I get a taxi? où est-ce que je peux trouver un taxi?
YOU MAY SEE ...
tête de station *taxi rank*
tea du thé
could I have a cup of tea? est-ce que je peux avoir un thé?
YOU MAY THEN HEAR ...
un thé citron? *tea with lemon*
un thé lait? *tea with milk*
» *TRAVEL TIP: tea is not automatically served with milk*
team l'équipe *f*
teamwork le travail d'équipe
technical technique
the technical departments les services techniques
technician un technicien
technology la technologie
telegram un télégramme
I want to send a telegram je veux envoyer un télégramme

telephone le téléphone
a (telephone) call une communication (téléphonique)
can I make a phone-call? est-ce que je peux téléphoner?
can I speak to ...? est-ce que je peux parler à ...?
I'll telephone you when I get back je vous appellerai à mon retour
as I mentioned on the telephone comme je le disais au téléphone
further to our recent telephone conversation suite à notre dernière conversation téléphonique
telephone directory l'annuaire du téléphone
» *TRAVEL TIP: you can phone from most cafés: pay at counter or you may have to buy a 'jeton' (token) which you insert in the pay phone; there are now more call boxes, esp. in Paris (grey colour): insert coin (50 centimes for local call) before lifting receiver; to dial the UK: 19 44+town prefix without the 0 (from Switzerland or Belgium: 00 44 etc); if you get somebody to call you back from the UK: 010 33 plus town prefix without the 0 (to Switzerland: 010 41 etc; to Belgium 010 32 etc); see numbers on pp. 188–189*
YOU MAY HEAR ...
qui est à l'appareil? *who's speaking?*
c'est un faux numéro *sorry wrong number*
la ligne est occupée *the line is engaged*
ne quittez pas, je vous passe ... *hold the line, I'm putting you through to ...*
television la télévision
on television à la télévision
telex un télex

by telex par télex
tell: **could you tell me where ...?** est-ce que vous pouvez me dire où ...?
could you tell him that ... est-ce que vous pourriez lui dire que ...?
as I told you at our last meeting comme je vous le disais à notre dernière réunion
as I told your colleague comme je l'ai dit à votre collègue
temperature la température
temporary temporaire
tender une offre, une soumission
we are interested in tendering for this contract nous comptons faire une soumission pour cette adjudication
invitation to tender un appel d'offres
terminate (*agreement*) résilier
termination (*cancellation*) une résiliation (*expiry*) l'expiration *f*
terminus le terminus
terms (*payment*) les modalités
what are your terms? quelles sont vos conditions?
improved terms des conditions améliorées
under the terms of the agreement suivant les termes du contrat
terrible terrible, affreux(-euse)
test un test
it's still being tested c'est encore à l'essai
TGV Train à Grande Vitesse: *Advanced Passenger Train*
» *TRAVEL TIP: very fast and very comfortable train (Paris-Lyon just over 2 hours, Paris-Genève around 4 hours, etc); 1st and 2nd class on all services; seat reservation is compulsory, but can be done at Gare de Lyon shortly before departure (automatic machines); there is an extra charge on some services*
than que

bigger/better than ... plus gros/meilleur que ...
thanks, thank you merci
thank you very much merci beaucoup
YOU MAY THEN HEAR ...
je vous en prie *you're welcome*
thank you for your letter merci de votre lettre
that ce(cette)
that man/plane cet homme/avion
I'd like that one j'aimerais celui-là(celle-là)
I think that ... je crois que ...
that was ... c'était ...
what about that? et ça?
the le(la), (*plural*) les
the airport l'aéroport
their *see* **my**
them: **I know them** je les connais
give them ... donnez-leur ...
will you give it to them? est-ce vous pouvez le(la) leur donner?
with them avec eux(elles)
then (*at that time*) à ce moment, alors
(*after that*) ensuite
(*therefore*) donc
there là
how do I get there? comment est-ce qu'on y va?
there is/there are ... il y a ...
is there/are there ...? est-ce qu'il y a ...?
there isn't/aren't any ... il n'y a pas de ...
there you are (*giving something*) voilà
these ces
can I take these? est-ce que je peux prendre ceux-ci(celles-ci)?
they ils(elles)

thick épais(se)
thin mince
thing une chose
I've lost all my things j'ai perdu toutes mes affaires
think: **I'll think it over** je vais y réfléchir
I think so je crois
I don't think so je ne crois pas
I think that ... je crois que ...
third troisième
thirsty: **I'm thirsty** j'ai soif
this ce(cette)
this man/plane cet homme/avion
can I have this one? est-ce que je peux avoir celui-ci(celle-ci)?
this is Mr ... je vous présente Monsieur ..., voici Monsieur ...
is this ...? est-ce que c'est ...?
those ces
how much are those? combien coûtent ceux-ci(celles-ci)?
through à travers
Thursday jeudi
ticket (*train, plane etc*) un billet
(*bus*) un ticket
(*cloakroom*) un ticket, un numéro
» *TRAVEL TIP: see* **bus, métro**
tie (*necktie*) une cravate
I'm tied up all day je suis pris toute la journée
I want to get all the details tied down je voudrais qu'on règle tous les détails
tiers *third, third party (or parties)*
tight (*schedule*) serré(e)
(*control*) sévère, strict(e)
(*margin*) étroit(e)
it's tight but I think we'll make it c'est juste mais je crois que nous y arriverons
tights des collants
timbres *stamps*

time: **what's the time?** quelle heure est-il?
at what time? à quelle heure?
this time cette fois
last time/next time la dernière/prochaine fois
3 times trois fois
3 times as fast trois fois plus vite
I haven't got time je n'ai pas le temps
for the time being pour le moment
it takes a lot of time ça prend beaucoup de temps
to arrive in time arriver à temps
to arrive on time arriver à l'heure
it's a question of time c'est une question de temps
we need more time nous avons besoin de plus de temps
we cannot give you any more time nous ne pouvons pas vous donner plus de temps
have a good time! amusez-vous bien!
time and motion study une étude des cadences
it's time-consuming ça prend du temps
HOW TO TELL THE TIME
it's one o'clock il est une heure
it's 2 am/pm il est deux heures du matin/de l'après-midi
at 7 pm à sept heures du soir
2.05 deux heures cinq
2.15 deux heures et quart
2.30 deux heures et demie
2.40 trois heures moins vingt
2.45 trois heures moins le quart

timetable (*travel*) un horaire
(*programme*) un calendrier

timing: **the timing of the payments** l'échelonnement des paiements

---

it's all a question of timing tout dépend du moment choisi
tip le pourboire
tiré *drawee*
tired: **I'm tired** je suis fatigué(e)
tireur *drawer*
tirez *pull*
tissues des Kleenex®
titre: au titre de ... *as ...*
titres *stock, securities*
to: **to England** en Angleterre
to Paris à Paris
give/show it to Mr ... donnez-/montrez-le à M. ...
tobacco du tabac
today aujourd'hui
a week/a month today dans une semaine/un mois
together ensemble
together with en même temps que, avec
can we pay all together? est-ce que nous pouvons payer tout ensemble?
toilet les toilettes
where are the toilets? où sont les toilettes?
tomato juice un jus de tomate
tomorrow demain
tomorrow morning/afternoon/evening demain matin/après-midi/soir
the day after tomorrow après-demain
a week tomorrow demain en huit
ton une tonne
» *1 ton=1,016 kilos*
tonic (water) un Schweppes®
tonight ce soir
tonne une tonne
» *1 tonne=1000 kilos=metric ton*
too aussi
too much/many (...) trop (de ...)
that's too much c'est trop

tool un outil
we are still tooling up nous en sommes encore au stade de la mise en train
tooth: **I've got toothache** j'ai mal aux dents
top: **on top of ...** en plus de ..., (*on*) sur
on the top floor au dernier étage
at the top en haut
top management les cadres supérieurs
our top salesman notre meilleur vendeur
topic un sujet
total le total
that makes a total of ... cela fait un total de ...
totally complètement
touch: **we'll get in touch with you** nous vous contacterons, nous prendrons contact avec vous
please get in touch with ... mettez vous en relation/rapport avec ...
please keep in touch restez en contact
if you could put me in touch with someone who ... si vous pouviez me mettre en rapport avec quelqu'un qui ...
tough (*competition etc*) serré(e), acharné(e) (*material*) solide, résistant(e)
towards vers
towel une serviette
town une ville
in town en ville
would you take me into town? est-ce que vous pouvez m'emmener en ville?
trade le commerce
people in the trade les spécialistes, les gens de la branche
trader un négociant, un marchand
trade secret un secret de fabrication
trade union un syndicat

---

trading deficit un déficit commercial
trading profit un bénéfice brut (d'exploitation)
trading surplus un surplus commercial
traditional traditionnel(le)
the traditional approach l'approche/la méthode traditionnelle
traffic lights les feux (de circulation)
train un train, **by train** en train
» *TRAVEL TIP: there are extra charges on some inter-city trains ('trains avec supplément')*
trainee un stagiaire
training l'apprentissage, la formation
training period un stage
traite *draft, bill*
tranquillizers des calmants
transbordement *transshipment*
transfer (*of money*) un virement
the sum has been transferred to your account la somme a été transférée sur votre compte
he's been transferred to the York branch il a été transféré à l'agence de York
transformer un transformateur
transhipment le transbordement
transit le transit
in transit en transit
damaged in transit abîmé en cours de route
transitaire *forwarding agent*
translate traduire
translation une traduction
would you translate that for me? est-ce que vous pouvez me traduire ça?
translator un traducteur(une traductrice)
transport le transport
has transport been arranged for us? est-ce que le problème des déplacements a été réglé?, est-ce qu'une voiture a été mise à notre disposition?
transport charges les frais de transport

travaux *works, roadworks*
travel voyager
travel agency une agence de voyage
traveller's cheque un chèque de voyage, un traveller's chèque
travelling salesman un voyageur de commerce
tremendous énorme
trend une tendance
trial (*in court*) un procès
 on a trial basis à l'essai
 trials are still being carried out les essais sont en cours
 trial order une commande à l'essai
 trial period une période d'essai
 trial run un essai
trip: **the trip out** l'aller
 the trip back le retour
 a short trip un court déplacement, un voyage de peu de durée
trouble des ennuis
 I'm having trouble with ... j'ai des ennuis avec ...
 that's just the trouble! c'est là le problème!
trouble-free sans problème
 no trouble pas de problème
trouble-shooter (*arbitrator*) un médiateur (*rescuer*) un expert (qui puisse sauver la situation, résoudre le problème)
trousers les pantalons
true vrai
 it's not true ce n'est pas vrai, c'est faux
trust: **I trust you** je vous fais confiance
 we have to trust each other nous devons nous faire mutuellement confiance
 it's based on trust c'est une question de confiance

trustworthy (*person*) digne de confiance
try essayer
we'll give it a try nous l'essaierons, nous allons essayer
please try to convince him essayez de le convaincre
TSVP Tournez S'il Vous Plaît: *pto*
TTC Toutes Taxes Comprises: *inclusive of tax*
Tuesday mardi
turn: **it's our turn to ...** c'est à nous de ...
as it turned out en fin de compte, finalement
turnover le chiffre d'affaires
(*of stock*) la rotation des stocks
an increase in turnover une augmentation du chiffre d'affaires
turn(a)round: **what sort of turn(a)round can you give us?** sous quels délais pouvez-vous le faire?
their turn(a)round time is too slow leurs délais sont trop longs
TVA Taxe à la Valeur Ajoutée: *VAT*
twice deux fois
twice as much deux fois plus
twin beds des lits jumeaux
type: **this type of ...** ce genre de ...
suitable for all types of ... convenant à tous les genres de ...
would you get this typed out for me? voulez-vous me taper ça, s'il vous plaît?
typewriter une machine à écrire
typical typique
typist une dactylo
ulcer un ulcère
umbrella un parapluie
unacceptable inacceptable
under sous
under 20% moins de 20%
under the terms of the contract conformément aux termes du contrat

undercapitalized sous-capitalisé
undercut: **we can undercut their prices** question prix, nous pouvons faire mieux qu'eux
underground (*rail*) le métro
underpaid sous-payé(e)
underpriced sous-évalué(e)
understaffed qui manque de personnel
understand comprendre
I don't understand je ne comprends pas
do you understand? est-ce que vous comprenez?
understanding: **if we can reach an understanding about ...** si nous pouvons nous entendre au sujet de ...
unexpected inattendu(e)
unfounded injustifié(e)
unhappy: **I'm still unhappy about it** ça ne me satisfait pas encore, ça ne me plaît toujours pas
union (*trade*) un syndicat
union member un syndiqué(une syndiquée)
unit l'unité
unit cost le coût unitaire
unit price le prix unitaire
United States les Etats-Unis
unless: **unless you can do it by next Wednesday** à moins que vous ne puissiez le faire d'ici à mercredi prochain
unlikely peu probable
until jusqu'à
until recently jusqu'à il n'y a pas longtemps
not until Tuesday pas avant mardi
unusual inhabituel
up: **sales are up 10%** les ventes ont augmenté de 10%
5% up on last year en augmentation de 5% sur l'année dernière

when the extra period is up à l'expiration du délai supplémentaire
up to yesterday/500 jusqu'à hier/500
he's not up yet il n'est pas encore levé
up-market haut de gamme
up-to-date moderne
to keep the records up to date mettre les dossiers à jour
will you bring me up to date on what's happening? est-ce que vous pouvez me mettre au courant des derniers évènements?
up-to-the-minute (*news, report*) de dernière heure
upturn une poussée, une relance
upwards: **the trend is still upwards** la tendance reste à la hausse
urgency: **please treat this as a matter of the greatest urgency** veuillez considérer ceci comme étant absolument prioritaire
urgent urgent(e)
us nous
use: **can I use ...?** est-ce que je peux utiliser ...?
useful utile
usine *factory*
usual: **the usual approach** la méthode habituelle
as usual comme d'habitude
usually d'habitude
U-turn (*in policy*) un demi-tour, une volte-face
vacancy (*job*) un poste vacant
valeur déclarée *value of contents*
valeurs *securities, assets*
valid valable
how long is it valid for? c'est valable combien de temps?
valuable: **the contents are valuable** le contenu a de la valeur
that's valuable advice ces conseils sont très utiles

that's valuable business cette commande (*etc*) vaut la peine
value la valeur
we value the work you've done nous apprécions le travail que vous avez fait
VAT la TVA (taxe à la valeur ajoutée)
vegetarian végétarien(ne)
vendeur *sales assistant, salesman, seller*
vendre: à vendre *for sale*
vente *sale*
verglas *ice (on road)*
verify (*check*) vérifier
versé *paid, paid up*
very très
very much better beaucoup mieux
I very much hope so je l'espère vraiment
vested interest un intérêt personnel
via via
view: in view of ... vu le(la) ..., étant donné le(la) ...
vintage year une bonne année
virages dangereux *dangerous bends*
virement *transfer*
visa un visa
visit (*noun*) une visite
on our last visit to your factory la dernière fois que nous avons visité votre usine
we look forward to M. Dupont's visit nous nous réjouissons de la visite prochaine de M. Dupont
vitesse limitée à: ... *maximum speed ...*
voice une voix
voie sans issue *cul-de-sac, no through road*
voie 6 *platform 6*
voltage le voltage
volume (*of production etc*) le volume

VRP Voyageurs, Représentants, Placiers: *travelling salespeople*
wagon-lit *sleeping car*
wagon-restaurant *dining car*
wait: **will we have to wait long?** est-ce qu'il faudra attendre longtemps?
don't wait for me ne m'attendez pas
I'm waiting for my colleague j'attends mon collègue
waiter le serveur, **waiter!** s'il vous plaît!
waitress la serveuse, **waitress!** s'il vous plaît!
wake: **will you wake me up at 7.30?** pouvez-vous me réveiller à sept heures et demie?
Wales le Pays de Galles
walk: **can we walk there?** est-ce qu'on peut y aller à pied?
wall le mur
wallet le portefeuille
want: **I want a ...** je voudrais un ...
I want to talk to ... je voudrais parler à ...
what do you want? qu'est-ce que vous voulez?
I don't want to je ne veux pas
he wants to ... il veut ...
they don't want to ils ne veulent pas
it's just what we want c'est exactement ce que nous voulons
warehouse un entrepôt
warehouse manager un responsable de magasin
warehousing costs les frais d'entreposage
warm chaud(e)
warning un avertissement
warranty une garantie
it's under warranty c'est sous garantie
was *see* **be**
wash: **can you wash these for me?** est-ce que vous pouvez me laver ça?
watch (*wrist–*) une montre
will you watch ...for me? est-ce que vous

pouvez surveiller ...?
watch out! attention!
water: **can I have some water?** est-ce que je peux avoir de l'eau?
way: **this is the way we see things developing** c'est ainsi que nous voyons l'évolution de la situation
let's do it this way faisons-le de cette façon, procédons de cette manière
OK, let's do it your way d'accord, faisons comme vous le voulez
this is the way forward c'est la bonne direction
the goods are on their way les marchandises sont en route
could you tell me the way to ...? quel est le chemin pour aller à ...?, pourriez-vous m'indiquer le chemin de ...?
waybill la lettre de voiture
we nous
weak faible
weather le temps
what filthy weather! quel sale temps!
Wednesday mercredi
week une semaine
a week today dans une semaine
a week tomorrow demain en huit
in a week dans une semaine
at the weekend (pendant) le weekend
weigh peser
weight le poids
welcome: **thank you for your warm welcome** merci de cet accueil chaleureux
welcome to ... bienvenue à ...
we would welcome your comments nous apprécierons vos commentaires

well bien
I'm not feeling well je ne me sens pas bien
he's not well il ne va pas bien
how are you? very well, thanks comment allez-vous? — très bien, merci
you speak English very well vous parlez très bien l'anglais
Welsh gallois(e)
were *see* **be**
west l'ouest
West Indian antillais(e)
West Indies les Antilles
wet mouillé(e)
what ... quel(quelle) ...?
what is that? qu'est-ce que c'est?
what's that in French? comment ça s'appelle en français?
what with? avec quoi?
what for? pourquoi?
when quand
when I arrived quand je suis arrivé
where: **where can we ...?** où est-ce que nous pouvons ...?
where is the post office? où est la poste?
YOU MAY THEN HEAR ...
près d'ici *nearby*, près de ... *close to* ...
très loin *a long way off*, tout droit *straight on*
à gauche, à droite *on the left, on the right*
prenez la première à gauche/droite *take first left/right*, après le feu rouge (les feux) *past the traffic lights*
whether si
which quel(quelle)
which one? lequel(laquelle)
YOU MAY THEN HEAR ...
celui-ci *this one*, celui-là *that one*
whisky du whisky
white blanc(blanche)
who qui

wholesale la vente en gros
wholesale price le prix de gros
wholesaler le grossiste
whose: **... whose company was ...** ... dont la société était ...
whose is this? à qui est ceci?
YOU MAY THEN HEAR ...
c'est à moi/lui/elle/eux
it belongs to me/him/her/them
why pourquoi, **why not?** pourquoi pas?
YOU MAY THEN HEAR ...
parce que ... *because*
wide large
width la largeur
wife: **my wife** ma femme
will: **when will it be finished?** quand est-ce que ce sera fini?
will you do it? est-ce que vous pouvez le faire?
I will come back je reviendrai
willing: **are you willing to ...?** est-ce que vous êtes prêts à ...?, est-ce que vous êtes d'accord de ...?
we are willing to try it nous sommes prêts à essayer
win (*competition*) gagner
(*order, contract*) obtenir, décrocher
window la fenêtre
(*of car*) la vitre
near the window près de la fenêtre
in the window (*shop*) dans la vitrine
windscreen le pare-brise
wine du vin
can I see the wine list? est-ce que je peux voir la carte des vins? (*see wine guide overleaf*)
red wine du vin rouge, **white wine** du vin blanc

REDS (vins rouges)
Bordeaux *areas*: Médoc, Graves, St Emilion; *wines*: Château-Lafite, Château-Margaux, Château-Latour, Pomerol; **Bourgogne** Passe-tout-Grain, Nuits-St Georges, Clos-Vougeot, Côte de Nuits-Village, Pommard, Volnay, Meursault, Pouilly-Fuissé, Mâcon; **Beaujolais** Beaujolais-Villages, Juliénas, Morgon, Moulin à Vent, Saint Amour; **Côtes du Rhône** Hermitage, Châteauneuf-du-Pape, Gigondas; **Suisse** Dôle

WHITES (vins blancs)
Bordeaux Sauternes, Graves, Barsac; **Bourgogne** Bourgogne Alligoté, Mâcon blanc; **Loire** Muscadet, Gros Plant, Anjou, Coteaux du Layon, Saumur; **Alsace** Silvaner, Riesling, Pinot Blanc, Tokay d'Alsace, Gewürztraminer, Edelzwicker; **Suisse** la Côte (Vaud): Vinzel; Lavaux (Vaud): St Saphorin, Yvorne; Valais: Fendant, Johannisberg
» *TRAVEL TIP: in Switzerland, you don't order 'un quart' (25cl), as in France, but 'un ballon' (10cl), 'deux décis' (20cl), 'trois décis' (30cl) or 'un demi' (0.5l)*

ROSE (vins rosés)
Rosé d'Anjou, Tavel (Côtes du Rhône), Rosé de Provence

CHAMPAGNE
Dom Pérignon, Moët et Chandon, Mumm, Veuve Clicquot, Piper Heidsieck, Pommery, Taittinger

a few wine terms
appellation contrôlée AOC *quality label: a guarantee that a wine comes from one particular area*, vin de pays *not AOC, but superior to 'vin ordinaire'*, sec *dry*, demi-sec *medium*, doux *sweet*, mousseux *sparkling*, fruité *fruity*

have you got something dry/sweeter? est-ce que vous avez quelque chose de sec/de plus doux?
what would you recommend with ...? que nous conseillez-vous avec ...?
cheers! santé!

winter l'hiver
wire (*electrical*) un fil électrique
wise (*policy, decision*) sage, prudent(e)
I think it would be wise to ... je crois qu'il serait prudent de ...
wish: **best wishes** meilleurs voeux
(*on letter*) meilleures pensées
please give my best wishes to M. Duval transmettez mes amitiés/salutations à M. Duval
Mr Gordon sends his best wishes M. Gordon vous envoie ses amitiés/salutations
the customer's wishes les souhaits du client
with avec
withdraw (*money from account*) retirer, tirer
if we withdraw from the project si nous nous retirons du projet
within: **within 3 months** d'ici trois mois, en trois mois
without sans
witness un témoin
will you act as a witness for me? pouvez-vous me servir de témoin?
woman une femme
wonderful merveilleux(-euse), magnifique
wood du bois
wool de la laine
word un mot
I don't know that word je ne connais pas ce mot
word processor un système de traitement de texte
work (*noun*) le travail
(*verb*) travailler
there's a lot of work to do il y a beaucoup à faire

---

it's very difficult work c'est un travail difficile
it's not working ça ne fonctionne pas (*plan*) ça ne marche pas
I work in London je travaille à Londres
a good working relationship une bonne relation de travail
if we can work something out si nous arrivons à arranger quelque chose
it'll work out in the end ça finira par marcher

workforce le personnel
working capital le capital d'exploitation
workload le travail (à faire)
works l'usine
workshop l'atelier
world le monde
the best in the world le meilleur du monde
worldwide (*distribution, sales*) mondial(e)
worry: **I'm worried about it** je suis inquiet à ce sujet, ça me préoccupe
don't worry ne vous inquiétez pas
worse: **it's worse** c'est pire
it's getting worse ça empire, ça s'aggrave
worst: **the worst** le pire
worth: **it's not worth that much** ça ne vaut pas autant
is it worthwhile going to ...? est-ce que ça vaut la peine d'aller à ...?
100F worth of ... pour cent francs de ...
worthless sans valeur
would: **would you send us ...?** pourriez-vous nous envoyer ...? *see also* **like**
wrap: **could you wrap it up?** pourriez-vous l'emballer?
to wrap up a deal conclure un marché
wrapping l'emballage *m*
write écrire
could you write it down? pouvez-vous me l'écrire?

I wrote it all down j'ai tout noté
we'll be writing to you nous vous écrirons
could we have that in writing? pourriez-vous nous le confirmer par écrit?
write off (*losses*) passer aux profits et pertes
writing paper du papier à lettres
wrong faux(fausse)
I think the invoice is wrong je crois qu'il y a une erreur dans la facture
there's something wrong with ... il y a quelque chose qui ne va pas dans ...
you're wrong vous avez tort, vous vous trompez
sorry, wrong number excusez-moi, je me suis trompé de numéro
yard *1 yard=91.44 cms=0.91 m*
year l'année *f*
yearly annuellement
yellow jaune
yellow pages les pages jaunes (de l'annuaire)
yes oui, **you can't — yes, I can** vous ne pouvez pas — si, je peux
yesterday hier
the day before yesterday avant-hier
yesterday morning/evening hier matin/soir
yet: **is it ready yet?** est-ce que c'est déjà prêt?
not yet pas encore
you vous
» *TRAVEL TIP: use the 'vous' form in most situations; the familiar 'tu' form is for people you know well; it's best to let the French speaker start using the 'tu' form; examples are*: vous parlez/tu parles (*regular*); vous venez/tu viens; vous prenez/tu prends (*note that the 'tu' form sounds the same as the 'je' form*); *see also* **my**
young jeune
your *see* **my**
Yugoslavia la Yougoslavie
zero zéro, **zero-rated** (*VAT*) sans TVA

0 zéro [zay-roh]
1 un [an]
2 deux [duh]
3 trois [trwah]
4 quatre [kahtr]
5 cinq [sank]
6 six [sees]
7 sept [set]
8 huit [weet]
9 neuf [nuhf]
10 dix [dees]
11 onze [onz]
12 douze [dooz]
13 treize [trayz]
14 quatorze [kah-torz]
15 quinze [kanz]
16 seize [sayz]
17 dix-sept [dee-set]
18 dix-huit [deez-weet]
19 dix-neuf [deez-nuhf]
20 vingt [vant]
21 vingt-et-un [van-tay-an]
22 vingt-deux [vant-duh]
23 vingt-trois [vant-trwah]
24 vingt-quatre [vant-kahtr]
25 vingt-cinq [vant-sank]
26 vingt-six [vant-sees]
27 vingt-sept [vant-set]
28 vingt-huit [vant-weet]
29 vingt-neuf [vant-nuhf]
30 trente [tront]
31 trente-et-un [tront-ay-an]
40 quarante [kah-ront]
50 cinquante [san-kont]
60 soixante [swah-sont]
70 soixante-dix [swah-sont-dees]
71 soixante-et-onze [swah-sont ay onz]
72 soixante-douze [swa-sont dooz]

» *TRAVEL TIP: in Switzerland and Belgium, 'septante' [sep-tont], 'septante et un', 'septante-deux' etc.*

80 quatre-vingts [kahtruh-van]
81 quatre-vingt un

1st premier [pruhm-yay], 1er
2nd deuxième [duhz-yem], 2ème, 2e
3rd troisième [trwahz-yem]
4th quatrième [kahtr-yem]
5th cinquième [sank-yem]
6th sixième [seez-yem]
7th septième [set-yem]
8th huitième [weet-yem]
9th neuvième [nuhv-yem]
10th dixième [deez-yem]
11th onzième [onz-yem]
12th douzième [dooz-yem]
13th treizième [trayz-yem]

82 quatre-vingt-deux
» *TRAVEL TIP: in parts of Switzerland and in Belgium, also 'huitante' [wee-tont], or 'octante' [ok-tont], 'huitante et un', 'huitante-deux' etc.*
90 quatre-vingt-dix
91 quatre-vingt-onze
92 quatre-vingt-douze
» *TRAVEL TIP: in Switzerland and Belgium, 'nonante' [nuh-nont], 'nonante et un', 'nonante-deux' etc.*
100 cent [son]
101 cent un [son an]
102 cent deux
175 cent soixante-quinze
200 deux cents
202 deux cent deux
1,000 mille [meel], 1.000, 1 000
2,000 deux mille, 2.000, 2 000
2,469 deux mille quatre cents soixante-neuf
1,000,000 un million [mee-yon], 1.000.000, 1 000 000
1,000,000,000 un milliard [mee-yahr]

$\frac{1}{4}$ un quart [khar], $\frac{3}{4}$ trois quarts
$\frac{1}{3}$ un tiers [tee-air], $\frac{2}{3}$ deux tiers
$\frac{1}{2}$ un demi [duh-mee], $1\frac{1}{2}$ un... et demi
$1\frac{1}{4}$ un... et quart
$\frac{1}{8}$ etc un huitième etc

0.2 zéro virgule [veer-gool] deux, 0,2
3.86 trois virgule quatre-vingt six, 3,86
Note that in French the comma is used as a decimal point and the full-stop is used for thousands as illustrated above.

4+4 quatre plus [ploos] quatre *or* et [ay] quatre
4−2 quatre moins [mwan] deux
4×4 quatre fois [fwah] quatre
4+4=8 quatre plus quatre égale [ay-gahl] huit
40% of 35 quarante pour cent [poor son] de trente-cinq
30% increase une augmentation de trente pour cent

2^2 deux au carré [kah-ray], deux à la puissance deux
2^3 deux au cube [koob], deux à la puissance trois
2^4 deux à la puissance [pwee-sons] quatre

Special Vocabulary List

English/Anglais	*French/Français*

Special Vocabulary List

English/Anglais	*French/Français*

CONTACTS LIST

Name	*Address*	*Tel.*